HIGHLANDS
AND ISLANDS

HIGHLANDS AND ISLANDS

A Collection of the Poetry of Place

Edited by
MARY MIERS

Introduced by
JOHN BYRNE

ELAND • LONDON

First published in April 2010 by Eland Publishing Ltd,
61 Exmouth Market, Clerkenwell, London EC1R 4QL

This arrangement and commentary © Mary Miers

ISBN 978 1 906011 29 1

Pages designed and typeset by Antony Gray
Cover image: Orkney Coast View by Sheila Scott
from the St Mary's Hospital Paddington
Art Collection/Bridgeman Art Library © Sheila Scott
Printed and bound in Spain by GraphyCems, Navarra

Contents

LORE

LOVE

LIGHT

For my godchildren
Fergus Wigan, Alexander Miers,
Matilda Ruck, Hannah Rogerson,
Hector Macdonald, Hugh Leckie,
Harry Goodwin and Alfie Hayes,
in memory of many happy
Hebridean days

Introduction

My first trip to the Highlands was in 1950 when I was ten. Prior to that I had never been further north than the Wee Imps Picture House at Paisley Road Toll near Ibrox. A number of us (we were about a dozen and a half, I think) from Our Lady of Lourdes Primary School in Glasgow were carried by train to Elgin, thence to nearby Hopeman, where we were put up in a drill hall and slept in bunk beds, of which we had only ever heard mention in such magazines as *The Saturday Evening Post*, and then only if we happened to be sitting in one of the more 'select' dentist's waiting rooms in my home town of Paisley. Yes, I know that Elgin isn't really the Highlands – more the north-east seaside – but I mention the school trip for the simple reason that I get to put on record the fact that, from the train as it puffed its way through the pine-forested lower reaches of northern Scotland, I saw the Monarch of the Glen! Or, perhaps, a near-relation – I couldn't be sure – but the fact is, it was utterly breathtaking, this happenchance, as I thought of it then. Like spotting a unicorn while standing at a bus stop. And, as all of my fellow-passengers were caught up in a game of pontoon, I had this unforgettable gone-in-a-flash magical moment all to myself!

Which, rather neatly, brings me round to introducing this anthology – no gone-in-a-flash 'magical' moments, nor, for that matter, 'Monarchs of the Glen', but poems in their stead. Thank the Lord and, more appropriately, Mary Miers, for her masterly selection of the material, and her concise and very un-dry intro-ductions to the poems/songs themselves. For me, *Highlands and*

Islands: Poetry of Place is both an education and a real delight. Among my favourites (these on one reading only – readers will discover their own treasures should they browse, dip, or peruse at leisure) are, in no particular order: George Mackay Brown's 'Hamnavoe' and (especially) 'The Kirk and the Ship'; Douglas Dunn's bone-bleak 'St Kilda's Parliament', Louis MacNeice's refreshingly acerbic 1937 take on island life in 'The Hebrides', Sorley MacLean's heart-haunting 'Hallaig', Alexander MacDonald's 'seditously' nationalistic paean to Highland attire, 'The Proud Plaid', Hamish Henderson's rip-snorting 'Ballad of the Men of Knoydart' and Wordsworth's 'The Solitary Reaper' (which I could almost recite by heart having learned it at St Mirin's Academy, but all the more welcome for that! A knockout, by anyone's reckoning.) And last, but by no stretch of the imagination least, Hugh MacDiarmid's 'The Little White Rose' – a gem, a masterpiece, a unicorn.

JOHN BYRNE
Edinburgh, 2010

LIFE

From the Gaelic-speaking crofter 'proud of his shyness and of his small life', to the choirs of seabirds squabbling and plummeting from the 'great sea-citadel' of St Kilda's cliffs, life in the Highlands and Islands has a millennial feel. Here, among the rocks and peat, along the arteries of river, road and sea, we glimpse patterns of existence that have endured through generations, the daily rituals of farmers and fishermen in concert with their natural environment, bound by the loyalties and lore of community and clan.

Happiness

by **MEG BATEMAN** (b.1959)

2002
Translated from the Gaelic by the poet

Often have I seen them come together,
two old friends, two crofters,
who after a brief murmured greeting
will stand wordlessly together,
side by side, not facing each other,
and look out on the land whose
ways and memories unite them,
breathe in the air, and the scent of
tobacco and damp and lamb scour,
in the certain knowledge that talk
would hamper that expansive communion,
break in on their golden awareness
of all there is between them.

Although not a native Gael, Meg Bateman seems to have an innate feel for the Hebridean temperament. She studied and taught classical Gaelic at the University of Aberdeen before moving to Skye, where she now teaches at the Gaelic college Sabhal Mòr Ostaig. As well as three collections of her own poetry, she has translated and edited anthologies of medieval and seventeenth-century Gaelic verse. This poem was commissioned by the BBC for National Poetry Day.

Gaelic Stories

by **IAIN CRICHTON SMITH** (1928–1998)

(Iain Mac a' Ghobhainn)

Published 1960

Translated from the Gaelic by the poet

1
A fisherman in Wellingtons
and his sweetheart
and his mother.

2
A story
about an old man
and a seal.

3
A woman
reading a Bible for seven years
waiting for a sailor.

4
A melodeon.
A peat stack.
An owl.

5
A croft.
Two brothers.
A plate with potatoes.

6
A girl from Glasgow
wearing a mini
in church.

7
The sea
and a drifter,
the Golden Rose.

8
A man who was in Australia
coming home
on a wedding night.

9
A romance
between cheese
and milk.

10
Glasgow
in a world of nylons
and of neon.

11
Two women
talking
in a black house.

12
A monster
rising from the sea,
'Will you take tea?'

13
A comedy
in a kitchen,
with jerseys.

14
A conversation
between a loaf and
cheese.

15
A conversation
between a Wellington
and a herring.

16
A conversation
between fresh butter
and a cup.

17
A conversation
between Yarmouth
and Garrabost.

18
A moon
hard and high
above a marsh.

Iain Crichton Smith was the son of a Hebridean merchant seaman
and a fisher-girl. He grew up in Lewis, went to Aberdeen University
and worked as a schoolmaster in Oban from 1955 to 1977, writing
prolifically in Gaelic and English throughout his life. His novel *The
Last Summer* (1969) is a thinly-veiled autobiographical account of
growing up in Lewis, where he experienced great richness, but also
felt utterly constrained by the narrow world of the Free Kirk. His
poetry can be stark and bleak – 'a repudiation of the Romantic
Sublime' – but he had an infectious sense of humour and much of
his work stands out for its 'stylistic sharpness, its questioning
intelligence, its easy going biculturalism and its wit'.

Hamnavoe

by **GEORGE MACKAY BROWN** (1921–96)

Published 1959

My father passed with his penny letters
Through closes opening and shutting like legends
   When barbarous with gulls
   Hamnavoe's morning broke

On the salt and tar steps. Herring boats,
Puffing red sails, the tillers
   Of cold horizons, leaned
   Down the gull-gaunt tide

And threw dark nets on sudden silver harvests.
A stallion at the sweet fountain
   Dredged water, and touched
   Fire from steel-kissed cobbles.

Hard on noon four bearded merchants
Past the pipe-spitting pier-head strolled,
   Holy with greed, chanting
   Their slow grave jargon.

A tinker keened like a tartan gull
At cuithe-hung doors. A crofter lass
   Trudged through the lavish dung
   In a dream of cornstalks and milk.

Blessings and soup plates circled. Euclidian light
Ruled the town in segments blue and gray.
   The school bell yawned and lisped
   Down ignorant closes.

In 'The Arctic Whaler' three blue elbows fell,
Regular as waves, from beards spumy with porter,
 Till the amber day ebbed out
 To its black dregs.

The boats drove furrows homeward, like ploughmen
In blizzards of gulls. Gaelic fisher girls
 Flashed knife and dirge
 Over drifts of herring.

And boys with penny wands lured gleams
From the tangled veins of the flood. Houses went blind
 Up one steep close, for a
 Grief by the shrouded nets.

The kirk, in a gale of psalms, went heaving through
A tumult of roofs, freighted for heaven. And lovers
 Unblessed by steeples, lay under
 The buttered bannock of the moon.

He quenched his lantern, leaving the last door.
Because of his gay poverty that kept
 My seapink innocence
 From the worm and black wind;

And because, under equality's sun,
All things wear now to a common soiling,
 In the fire of images
 Gladly I put my hand
 To save that day for him.

George Mackay Brown's elegiac poem in memory of his father, a postman who died in 1940, is the fourth of six versions written over more than forty years. It is also a celebration of the poet's hometown, Stromness in Orkney, which he refers to in his writings by its old Norse name of Hamnavoe (haven bay). Moving processionally through a typical day, the poet constructs a series of images that vividly convey the life of this remote community, with its characters and daily rituals. He lived in a council house just round from the harbour and every Thursday for a number of years published a short essay in *The Orcadian* entitled 'Letter from Hamnavoe', which he described as 'walks out of doors in all weathers. You meet this neighbour, that friend, and linger and gossip a little about the weather and the old days; drop into a shop for tobacco, maybe; look over a garden wall at green things growing. The sound of the sea is everywhere.'

In the Highlands

by ROBERT LOUIS STEVENSON (1850–1894)

1869–70

In the highlands, in the country places,
Where the old plain men have rosy faces,
  And the young fair maidens
   Quiet eyes;
Where essential silence cheers and blesses,
And for ever in the hill-recesses
  Her more lovely music
   Broods and dies –

O to mount again where erst I haunted;
Where the old red hills are bird-enchanted,
  And the low green meadows
   Bright with sward;

And when even dies, the million-tinted,
And the night has come, and planets glinted,
    Lo, the valley hollow
        Lamp-bestarr'd!

O to dream, O to awake and wander
There, and with delight to take and render,
    Through the trance of silence,
        Quiet breath!
Lo! for there, among the flowers and grasses,
Only the mightier movement sounds and passes;
    Only winds and rivers,
        Life and death.

This was probably inspired by Stevenson's trips to the Highlands and Islands in 1868–70, when he was a trainee civil engineer. A son of the famous Stevenson dynasty of lighthouse builders, he visited the family firm's harbour works at Wick in 1868, and the following year accompanied his father on a tour of lighthouses in Orkney and the Shetlands; then in 1870 he spent three weeks on Earraid, the tiny isle off Mull that features in *Kidnapped*, on which the shore works for Dhu Heartach lighthouse were based.

The Hebrides

by **LOUIS MACNEICE** (1907–1963)

1937

On those islands
The West-Wind drops its messages of indolence,
No one hurries, the Gulf Stream warms the gnarled
Rampart of gneiss, the feet of the peasant years
Pad up and down their sentry-beat not challenging
Any comer for the password − only Death
Comes through unchallenged in his general's cape.
The houses straggle on the umber moors,
The Aladdin lamp mutters in the boarded room
Where a woman smoors the fire of fragrant peat.
No one repeats the password for it is known,
All is known before it comes to the lips –
Instinctive wisdom. Over the fancy vases
The photos with the wrinkles taken out,
The enlarged portraits of the successful sons
Who married wealth in Toronto or New York,
Cajole the lonely evenings of the old
Who live embanked by memories of labour
And child-bearing and scriptural commentaries.
On those islands
The boys go poaching their ancestral rights –
The Ossianic salmon who take the yellow
Tilt of the river with a magnet's purpose –
And listen breathless to the tales at the ceilidh
Among the peat-smoke and the smells of dung
That fill the felted room from the cave of the byre.

No window opens of the windows sunk like eyes
In a four-foot wall of stones casually picked
From the knuckly hills on which these houses crawl
Like black and legless beasts who breathe in their sleep
Among the piles of peat and pooks of hay –
A brave oasis in the indifferent moors.
And while the stories circulate like smoke,
The sense of life spreads out from the one-eyed house
In wider circles through the lake of night
In which articulate man has dropped a stone –
In wider circles round the black-faced sheep,
Wider and fainter till they hardly crease
The ebony heritage of the herded dead.
[. . .]
On those islands
The black minister paints the tour of hell
While the unregenerate drink from the bottle's neck
In gulps like gauntlets thrown at the devil's head
And spread their traditional songs across the hills
Like fraying tapestries of fights and loves,
The boar-hunt and the rope let down at night –
Lost causes and lingering home-sickness.
On those islands
The fish come singing from the drunken sea,
The herring rush the gunwales and sort themselves
To cram the expectant barrels of their own accord –
Or such is the dream of the fisherman whose wet
Leggings hang on the door as he sleeps returned
From a night when miles of net were drawn up empty.
On those islands
A girl with candid eyes goes out to marry
An independent tenant of seven acres

Who goes each year to the south to work on the roads
In order to raise a rent of forty shillings,
And all the neighbours celebrate their wedding
With drink and pipes and the walls of the barn reflect
The crazy shadows of the whooping dancers.
[. . .]

Dedicated to his friend Hector MacIver, the writer and broadcaster who advised MacNeice on his itinerary for visiting the Outer Hebrides in 1937, this poem comes at the end of *I Crossed the Minch* (1938), which MacNeice described as 'a tripper's book, written by someone who was disappointed and tantalised by the islands and seduced by them only to be reminded that on that soil he will always be an outsider. I doubt if I shall visit the Western Islands again'. MacNeice's book certainly provides a refreshing counterbalance to the sentimentalising, purple prose churned out by so many Highland enthusiasts at the time. Grumpy and elated in turns, he advises his reader not to follow him out to the Outer Isles: 'The natives will not welcome you enthusiastically. They will be polite, considerate and hospitable, but they will be able to get along better without you; they have not yet acquired the Blackpool mentality'. Appalled by the food and damp hotel beds, and alienated by his lack of Gaelic, he veers between 'wonder and boredom, exuberance and melancholy' in his quest for the real people, customs and landscape of the Hebrides. The book is a hybrid mix: poems, imagined conversations, and some memorable passages of perfectly pitched prose that convey far better than many more enthusiastic accounts a world that has now all but disappeared.

St Kilda's Parliament

by **DOUGLAS DUNN** (b.1942)

The Photographer revisits his picture
1979

This poem was inspired by a widely reproduced photograph
showing the male population of St Kilda in the late nineteenth
century. They are seen lining 'the street' of Village Bay on Hirta,
the principal settlement of the four islands that make up the
astonishing archipelago of jagged cliffs and sea stacs which loom
out of the Atlantic 41 miles west of North Uist. 'This Parliament
meets daily, discusses the weather and the state of the sea etc. in a
few Gaelic phrases; and by a majority the order of the day is fixed,
and no single individual takes it upon himself to arrange his own
business until after they unitedly decide what is best' recorded
a contemporary account, perpetuating the idea of a St Kilda
'parliament', which a new book, *The Truth About St Kilda* (2010),
now reveals to be an exaggeration.

The photograph was taken in 1886 by Norman MacLeod,
colleague of George Washington Wilson, whose photographic
company acquired it in 1902. He took several views of the islanders
in their unique environment. All around the village still today,
strewn across the hillside, lie hundreds of cleitean, the small,
drystone huts in which they stored their produce. They lived off
seabirds: fulmars, gannets and puffins caught on the cliffs with
remarkable fowling skills, harvesting them for their oil, flesh, eggs
and feathers, and as payment in lieu of rent to their Macleod
landlords; everything was jointly owned. In the nineteenth century,
the St Kildans became an object of curiosity and boatloads of
tourists began to stop by. Increasingly, their independence was

undermined and life became unsustainable, with further damage wrought by the puritanical regime imposed by incoming clergymen. Eventually, in 1930, the last thirty-six islanders were evacuated at their own request and St Kilda, which had been occupied since the Early Bronze Age, lost for ever its native community.

On either side of a rock-paved lane
Two files of men are standing barefooted,
Bearded, waistcoated, each with a tam-o'-shanter
On his head, and most with a set half-smile
That comes from their companionship with rock,
With soft mists, with rain, with roaring gales,
And from a diet of solan goose and eggs,
A diet of dulse and sloke and sea-tangle,
And ignorance of what a pig, a bee, a rat,
Or rabbit look like, although they remember
The three apples brought here by a traveller
Five years ago, and have discussed them since.
And there are several dogs doing nothing
Who seem contemptuous of my camera,
And a woman who might not believe it
If she were told of the populous mainland.
A man sits on a bank by the door of his house,
Staring out to sea and at a small craft
Bobbing there, the little boat that brought me here,
Whose carpentry was slowly shaped by waves,
By a history of these northern waters.
Wise men or simpletons – it is hard to tell –
But in that way they almost look alike
You also see how each is individual,
Proud of his shyness and of his small life
On this outcast of the Hebrides

With his eyes full of weather and seabirds,
Fish, and whatever morsel he grows here.
Clear, too, is manhood, and how each man looks
Secure in the love of a woman who
Also knows the wisdom of the sun rising,
Of weather in the eyes like landmarks.
Fifty years before depopulation –
Before the boats came at their own request
To ease them from their dying babies –
It was easy, even then, to imagine
St Kilda return to its naked self,
Its archeology of hazelraw
And footprints stratified beneath the lichen.
See, how simple it all is, these toes
Playfully clutching the edge of a boulder.
It is a remote democracy, where men,
In manacles of place, outstare a sea
That rattles back its manacles of salt,
The moody jailer of the wild Atlantic.
[…]
Look at their sly, assuring mockery.
They are aware of what we are up to
With our internal explorations, our
Designs of affluence and education.
They know us so well, and are not jealous,
Whose be-all and end-all was an eternal
Casual husbandry upon a toehold
Of Europe, which, when failing, was not their fault.
You can see they have already prophesised
A day when survivors look across the stern
Of a departing vessel for the last time
At their gannet-shrouded cliffs, and the farewells

Of the St Kilda mouse and St Kilda wren
As they fall into the texts of specialists,
Ornithological visitors at the prow
Of a sullenly managed boat from the future.
They pose for ever outside their parliament,
[…]

Gannet

by EDWIN MORGAN (b.1920)

Published 1997

High the cliffs, and
blue the sky, and
mad the spray, and
bright the sun, and
deep as the grave
the teeming waters
never at rest
in St Kilda's cauldron.
Fish for the taking
lazing in innocence
island to island,
flesh for a thunderbolt
not thrown by gods,
not a Greek, not a Gael.
If the fish could look up:
a bird left the crag
white against the blue,
half hovered, half circled,

stopped in an air-path
with eye unblinking,
folded its wings, and
gravity-batteried,
sharp beak down, and
sharp tail up, it
plunged, it
plummeted, it
hit the sea, it
shot right under, and
vanished except
to the fish it speared
in a fearful irruption
from a heaven unseen.
So who is safe?
The gannet cliffs
are shrieking, but
not about that.

The St Kildans lived off young gannets (*guga*), harvesting the seabirds, along with fulmars and puffins, from the dizzying cliff face. In September, an annual massacre of the birds took place on Boreray, four miles north east of the main island of Hirta, and they returned in the spring to gather eggs. For generations of Ness men, too, catching guga from the remote rock of Sula Sgeir forty miles out from the northern tip of Lewis has been part of life for hundreds of years and is still an annual tradition. A mesmerising account is given in Donald Murray's book *The Guga Hunters* (2008). The bird is usually skinned, feathers and all, so that plucking is unnecessary, and the meat, salted and boiled, is considered a delicacy.

Midge

by **EDWIN MORGAN** (b. 1920)

Published 1997

The evening is perfect, my sisters.
The loch lies silent, the air is still.
The sun's last rays linger over the water
and there is a faint smirr, almost a smudge
of summer rain. Sisters, I smell supper,
and what is more perfect than supper?
It is emerging from the wood,
in twos and threes, a dozen in all,
making such a chatter and a clatter
as it reaches the rocky shore,
admiring the arrangements of the light.
See the innocents, my sisters,
the clumsy ones, the laughing ones,
the rolled-up sleeves and the flapping shorts,
there is even a kilt (god of the midges,
you are good to us!) So gather your forces,
leave your tree-trunks, forsake the rushes,
fly up from the sour brown mosses
to the sweet flesh of face and forearm.
Think of your eggs. What does the egg need?
Blood, and blood. Blood is what the egg needs.
Our men have done their bit, they've gone,
it was all they were good for, poor dears. Now
it is up to us. The egg is quietly screaming
for supper, blood, supper, blood, supper!
Attack, my little Draculas, my Amazons!

look at those flailing arms and stamping feet.
They're running, swatting, swearing, oh they're hopeless.
Keep at them, ladies. This is a feast.
This is a midsummer night's dream.
Soon we shall all lie down filled and rich,
and lay, and lay, and lay, and lay, and lay.

This is my favourite of the various poems dedicated to the tiny, infuriating, bloodsucking, itch-inducing *Culicoides Impunctatus*, the insect whose presence from June to September is an indelible part of Highland life. The midge in Gaelic is a *meanbh-chuileag* (tiny fly), and it is interesting to note the connection that appears to exist phonetically between the Gaelic *cuileag* and the Latin *culicoides*.

The Daft Hill Plover
(Feadag Ghòrach an t-Slèibhe)

by GEORGE CAMPBELL HAY (1915–84)

1947

> The daft hill plover tumbles,
> and cries his birling cry,
> tumbles and climbs and tumbles,
> daft in the wide hill-sky.
> Alone with his hill-top daftness,
> he runs himself a race,
> The windy, daft hill plover,
> daft with wind and space.

Taking for his title a Gaelic air, George Campbell Hay captures brilliantly that exhilarating sense of being wired to nature while walking across open moorland, ears filled with wind and the sharp, lonely alarm-call cry of the Golden Plover darting up and agitating overhead.

The son of a Renfrewshire minister, Campbell Hay spent much of his earlier life in Kintyre, where he learnt Gaelic in his teens. After graduating from Oxford in 1938 he threw himself into Scottish Nationalism. He served during the War in North Africa and Italy, where he produced some of his finest work. But an incident in Macedonia in 1946 left him severely traumatised, and thereafter he endured a long twilight life of mental illness and alcoholism. Despite this, he was a prolific and versatile linguist and translated and published poetry in numerous languages.

Roads

by **GEORGE MACKAY BROWN** (1921–96)

Published 1971

The road to the burn
Is pails, gossip, gray linen.

The road to the shore
Is salt and tar.

We call the track to the peats
The kestrel road.

The road to the kirk
Is a road of silences.

Ploughmen's feet
Have beaten a road to the lamp and barrel.

And the road from the shop
Is loaves, sugar, paraffin, newspapers, gossip.

Tinkers and shepherds
Have the whole round hill for a road.

The River

by JULIA WIGAN (b.1961)

2009

From deep hollows
I am born.
Steel-clear on a slime
Of green sphagnum.
I am here, holding nothing.

My seeps take in rain.
Swollen enough to dare
A cut through soft turf.
Strangers' hills let water drop.
My water holds their water.

With my new, heaving
Weight, I boast my way.
Drive over the falls and
Rear up behind an ancient rock.
I split round the sides and hold my might.

Calm down on the flats and
Gulp by the overhangs.
Take a rest on the slow bends.
Ducks suck webbed feet out of my mud flanks.
Cows slip their lips into my pools.
Cold fish hang in the sway.
I hold their cradles of spawn.

Gulls crack the sky,
Mad with scavenging.

I hear waters sucking at
Beaches more vast than mine.
I know I am near.
I can hold no more.

My banks have loosened
Their hold. I seep wide.
Ride with the trawlermen,
In their orange coats,
Holding onto our lives.

My life is dying but,
Up in the deep hollows,
I am being born.

Brought up in Santiago, Nairobi, Paris and London, Julia Wigan has
lived for the past twenty years in a remote part of Sutherland with
her husband and four children. She was inspired for this poem by
the River Friadh, a tributary of the Helmsdale.

Everlasting Sailing

by **DERICK THOMSON** (b.1921)

(Ruaraidh MacThòmais)

Published 2007
Translated from the Gaelic by the poet

> Alasdair Chaluim Alasdair
> and Niall Iain Ruaidh
> sail the seas still
> with their cheeks chipped
> by the wind's chisels,
> and with a salt smirr
> on their beard bristles,
> kindly eyes
> catching glimpses of eternity,
> the warm home
> beyond the storm,
> Jordan and Jerusalem,
> and Mùirneag/the loved one awaiting.

Poet's footnote: 'Alasdair Chaluim Alasdair and Niall Iain Ruaidh –
respectively from Swordale and Leurbost in Lewis – were well-known
skippers in the earlier part of the twentieth century. Alasdair's boat
was the Mùirneag [the hill that dominates the northern part of Lewis,
in Gaelic: darling, beloved woman; affectionate/tender girl], the last
sail-herring-boat to survive, and Niall was a first cousin of my
mother.'

LAND

The mountain and water landscapes of the Highlands and Islands have generated a tumult of passions and politics right up to the present day. This section contains poems of stirring intensity composed by native Gaels and incomers alike: reflections in different keys on the wild grandeur of the scenery; nostalgic laments for homeland by those in exile; expressions of fierce pride in attachment to land struggled and fought over for centuries; patriotic assertions of national identity. The importance of land to the Highlander – that lonely, wind-honed, unyielding yet incomparably beautiful terrain – cannot be underestimated. It is a bitter-sweet relationship, dominated for centuries by the emotive issue of land ownership, with the battle against the landlord ever to the fore.

Perfect

by HUGH MACDIARMID (1892–1978)

Published 1939

On the Western Seaboard of South Uist
(Los muertos abren los ojos a los que viven*)

I found a pigeon's skull on the machair,
All the bones pure white and dry, and chalky,
But perfect,
Without a crack or a flaw anywhere.

At the back, rising out of the beak,
Were twin domes like bubbles of thin bone.
Almost transparent, where the brain had been
That fixed the tilt of the wings.

This poem appears in the Author's Note at the beginning of his book *The Islands of Scotland*, preceded by the following passage: 'I do not envy any visitor to the Scottish islands who . . . responds to the typical sights and sounds of the islands on a lower plane than I take in the following poem, which owes its title to my recognition that the proper main object of recourse to islands . . . is, or ought to be, perfection'.

* The dead open the eyes of the living

Caledonia

by JAMES HOGG (1770–1835)

c.1800

Caledonia! thou land of the mountain and rock;
Of the ocean, the mist, and the wind:
Thou land of the torrent, the pine, and the oak;
Of the roebuck, the hart, and the hind:
Though bare are thy cliffs, and though barren thy glens;
Though bleak thy dun islands appear;
Yet kind are the hearts, and undaunted the clans,
That roam on those mountains so drear.

Thou land of the bay, and the head-land so steep;
Of the eagle, that hovers on high
O'er the still lake, where, etch'd on its bosom, asleep
Lie the mountain, the cloud, and the sky.
Thou land of the valley, the moor, and the hill;
Of the storm, and the proud rolling wave;
Yes, thou art the land of fair liberty still!
And the land of my forefathers' grave.

A foe from abroad, or a tyrant at home,
Could never thy ardour restrain;
The invincible bands of imperial Rome
Assay'd thy proud spirit in vain.
Firm seat of religion, of valour, of truth,
Of genius unshackled and free;
The Muses have left all the vales of the south,
My lov'd Caledonia, for thee.

Continuing the tradition of Burns and other revivalists who collected and re-worked old fragments into new compositions, the self-styled 'Ettrick Shepherd' wrote a vast number of songs. It is not known when he composed this one, but in 1804 he happened to hear an actor singing it, along with one of his other patriotic songs, in a Lancaster theatre. It first appeared in print in 1810, published in *The Forest Minstrel* at a time in Hogg's life when the folk tradition of his Border upbringing converged with the politer, more national-minded culture of the Edinburgh literati. Hogg had visited the Highlands by 1792 and returned a number of times. Here he uses Highland images to champion Scotland's national identity at a time of political uncertainty, when the threat of French invasion loomed.

Moladh Beinn Dòbhrain
(*The Praise of Ben Dorain*)

by DUNCAN BÀN MACINTYRE (1724–1812)
(Donnchadh Bàn Mac an t-Saoir)

Composed between 1751 and 1766
Translated from the Gaelic by Ronald Black

[. . .]

Ground The prize above each ben
   Is Ben Dorain's,
 Of all I've ever seen
   To me she was loveliest:
 Moorland long and smooth,
 Store where deer were found,

The brightness of the slope
        Is what I pointed to;
Groves of branching trees,
Woods containing grass:
Well-favoured is the stock
        That makes its dwelling there,
A white-buttocked band
With hunt pursuing them –
Lovely to me is the herd
        That were snuffle-nosed.
[. . .]
The means to put him to death
Is a man who'd be brave,
A gun well trimmed
        In a young man's grip,
A flint with a notch,
A screw in its top,
A cock that would strike it
        Hard on the hammers,
A trusty eight-sided barrel,
A stock of faultless wood
That would wound the slim stag
        And disable him –
With a man whose profession
        Was devoted to these,
Who despite them could master them
        With his devices.
[. . .]
Variation The small tapering hind
        Would be keenest in snuffing
With her sharp pointed nostril
        Seeking the wind:

Short-tailed and clean-limbed
Round the rocks of the mountain –
For terror of fire
            She stays up in the wilderness.
[. . .]
It's the wild-headed stag
With the white waxy rump,
Antlered and high-headed
            And noisy of roaring,
Who lives on Ben Dorain
            And knows all its crannies.
Yes, in Ben Dorain –
            Hard I'd find it to tell
How many high-headed stags
            Dwell in that hunting-ground;
A slim-footed hind
Followed by her calves
With their little white scuts
            Ascending a pass –
Up the rim of Coir' Chruiteir
Go the spiky-horned band.
When she stretches her legs
And goes at a gallop
Just the tips of her hooves
            Ever trample the ground:
Of all the men in the kingdom
Who could possibly follow her?
[. . .]

Much of Duncan Bàn Macintyre's earlier life was spent as a game-keeper among the Glenorchy hills, and this was composed when he was living at the foot of Ben Dorain near Bridge of Orchy. The poet-hunter was uneducated in the modern sense of reading and writing, but for his own language and tradition the oral education he got at his mother's knee in the ceilidh-houses of Glenorchy more than made up for that. The Rev. Donald MacNicol wrote down his work from oral recitation and a first edition of his poetry was published in 1768. Macintyre later migrated to Edinburgh, but he was at his best in his native hills, where his close affinity with nature and powers of observation produced 'a cataract of images' conveyed in beautiful passages of naturalistic description that remind one of early Irish nature poetry. *Moladh Beinn Dòbhrain* is a metaphor for the relationship of the Highlander to his land, composed at a time of territorial instability. In contrast to the exalted status of Nature and natural beauty as viewed by the Romantics, Gaelic poetry takes an inclusive view, emphasising the natural order of the landscape, where people and creatures all have their place. The huntsmen and deer belong to Ben Dorain, the hill belongs to them. The poem is composed of movements in alternating measures, intending to correspond with the variations of the pibroch (*pìobaireachd*), the classical music of the bagpipe.

Scotland Small?

by **HUGH MACDIARMID** (1892–1978)

Published 1974

Scotland small? Our multiform, our infinite Scotland small?
Only as a patch of hillside may be a cliché corner
To a fool who cries 'Nothing but heather!' where in September
    another
Sitting there and resting and gazing round
Sees not only the heather but blueberries
With bright green leaves and leaves already turned scarlet
Hiding ripe blue berries; and amongst the sage-green leaves
Of the bog-myrtle the golden flowers of the tormentil shining;
And on the small bare places, where the little Blackface sheep
Found grazing, milkworts blue as summer skies;
And down in neglected peat-hags, not worked
Within living memory, sphagnum moss in pastel shades
Of yellow, green, and pink; sundew and butterwort
Waiting with wide-open sticky leaves for their tiny winged prey;
And nodding harebells vying in their colour
With the blue butterflies that poise themselves delicately upon
    them;
And stunted rowans with harsh dry leaves of glorious colour.
'Nothing but heather!' – How marvellously descriptive! And
    incomplete!

Also published separately, this poem belongs to the first of Mac-
Diarmid's three prose poems combined under the title *Direadh*
(meaning the act of ascending) in 1974. From the vantage point of a
mountain the poet surveys his country, observes its multi-facetted

character brought together in a kaleidoscopic unity. This poem is a subtle assertion of national identity through the closely observed description of a specific landscape – one clearly transformed by the Highland Clearances. The land has been laid bare yet, on closer observation, see how it abounds with life.

The son of a rural postman, the fiery and controversial Hugh MacDiarmid (born Christopher Murray Grieve, adopted his pseudonym 1922) reacted against his Presbyterian upbringing and became an anti-establishment journalist and poet. To disassociate his work from English (he listed Anglophobia among his hobbies), he embarked on a 'creative engagement' with the Scots vernacular and developed his own version of lyrics based on the dialects of the Lowlands. He returned to writing poetry in English in 1934, while living in Shetland, where he composed some of his finest works. In 1928, he co-founded the National Party of Scotland, but he then joined the Communist party in 1934. Polemical and cantankerous, MacDiarmid was fond of a dram and 'liked to call a spade a shovel'. But those who knew him well like to recall his other, quieter side and wicked sense of humour.

The Hebrides

by JAMES G. WATSON

1920s

Dear golden isles!
Gold with the setting sun's last, purest glow,
Ruddy and purple with the heather's bloom,
Grey with grey mist;
Edged here with yellow sand and salt-blue grass,

There with red rocks and mounting crags whereon
The foam-dewed cushions of the sea-pinks cling.
Islands of heaving waves, and dancing boats,
And searching, jocund wind that shouts and sings
O'er fresh-blown summits, rushing east to meet
The soaring peaks and blending hills of Ross;
A living wind, the Grey Wind of the West,
That learns its secrets from the eternal sea,
And all its joy from the sea's myriad mirth.
And thence, perhaps, the dwellers in the isles
Their far-seeing eyes possess, and comely grace,
And their strange knowledge of the Hidden Things.
Lone, happy isles! Though over-learned fools
Prate of 'subsidence' and a 'sunken land'
It is not so; but long since, ere their fall
A blessed band of spirits held these isles,
Fulfilled a perfect life of perfect love,
And all was peace.

But I have seen you in far other mood,
Have heard the wild west wind
Wailing across the wide Atlantic plains,
To charge the waters with its own blind grief;
Whispering, sighing; then in sudden rage
Shrieking in ghostly madness, till the waves,
Roused by the immemorial grief that wraps
Each barren crag and islet, every yard
Of sandy machair, were themselves confused
With sorrow, nameless, old, whereof long since
They had forgot the cause; yet still were grieved,
And in despair raised yearning hoary heads,
Restless and joyless to the end of time.
O! it was like

The mourning of a troop of love-starved spirits!
The clinging mist was like their clinging hands,
And every islet was a devil's home!
And I have heard strange tales, how in the mist,
Lured by the kelpie's voice far from the shore,
Oarsmen for hours have wandered o'er the sea;
And how, whene'er they neared the saving land,
Foul creeping hands would seize and pull the boat,
Until the mad grey Terror clutched their souls
And they were swallowed by the waiting waves!

Nay, you are not all fair; and yet, and yet
There is – I know not what, some witching spell
That draws, and draws again; and whoso'er
Has tasted once the sea-weed's tang, and seen
The fairy-painted hills and yellow sand,
He must return again and yet again,
Nor even hope to break the glamorous band.

This was written by a seventeen-year-old pupil at Edinburgh's Royal High School and published in 1930 in *The Door of Youth; A Selection of Poems from Edinburgh Schools Magazines* with a foreword by John Buchan. Old fashioned and misted by the Celtic Twilight, it is nonetheless an impressive work for a teenager, capturing something that still resonates strongly with visitors to the islands today.

The Lord of the Isles

by SIR WALTER SCOTT (1771–1832)

1815

Loch Coruisk (*coir' uisg* – cauldron-water) was considered the *ne plus ultra* of the Romantic Sublime. Ringed by the jagged ramparts of the Cuillin, this remote loch, still accessible only by boat or on foot, is an awesome sight that can be elating or overpowering depending on mood. Walter Scott, who first visited the Hebrides in 1810 and returned in 1814 on a tour with a party of Northern Lighthouse commissioners (described in his *A Cruise Around Scotland in 1814*), describes it here in the last of his long romantic narrative poems. It is Spring 1307 and the fugitive Robert the Bruce, who has returned to assert his claim to the Scottish crown, has been reconciled with Ronald, Lord of the Isles, who is in love with his sister and has sworn fealty to him. They land on Skye and set off on foot to 'strike a mountain deer'.

Excerpt from Canto third

> To favouring winds they gave the sail,
> Till Mull's dark headlands scarce they knew
> And Ardnamurchan's hills were blue.
> But then the squalls blew close and hard,
> And, fain to strike the galley's yard,
>   And take them to the oar,
> With these rude seas, in weary plight,
> They strove the livelong day and night,
> Nor till the dawning had a sight
>   Of Skye's romantic shore.
> Where Coolin stoops him to the west,

They saw upon his shivered crest
    The sun's arising gleam;
But such the labour and delay,
Ere they were moored in Scarigh bay,
(For calmer heaven compelled to stay,)
    He shot a western beam.
Then Ronald said, – 'If true mine eye
These are the savage wilds that lie
North of Strathnardill and Dunskye;
    No human foot comes here,
And, since these adverse breezes blow,
If my good Liege love hunter's bow,
What hinders that on land we go,
    And strike a mountain deer?
[. . .]
No marvel thus the Monarch spake;
    For rarely human eye has known
A scene so stern as that dread lake,
    With its dark ledge of barren stone.
Seems that primeval earthquake's sway
Hath rent a strange and shattered way
    Through the rude bosom of the hill,
And that each naked precipice,
Sable ravine and dark abyss,
    Tells of the outrage still.
The wildest glen, but this, can show
Some touch of Nature's genial glow;
On high Benmore green mosses grow,
And heath-bells bud in deep Glencoe,
    And copse on Cruchan-Ben,
But here, above, around, below,
    On mountain or in glen,

Nor tree, nor shrub, nor plant, nor flower,
Nor aught of vegetative power,
  The weary eye may ken.
For all is rocks at random thrown,
Black waves, bare crags, and banks of stone,
  As if were here denied
The summer sun, the spring's sweet dew,
That clothe with many a varied hue
  The bleakest mountain-side.

And wilder, forward as they wound,
Were the proud cliffs and lake profound.
Huge terraces of granite black
Afforded rude and cumbered track;
  For from the mountain hoar,
Hurled headlong in some night of fear,
When yelled the wolf and fled the deer,
  Loose crags had toppled o'er;
And some, chance-poised and balanced, lay,
So that a stripling arm might sway
  A mass no host could raise,
In Nature's rage at random thrown,
Yet trembling like the Druid's stone
  On its precarious base.
The evening mists, with ceaseless change,
Now clothed the mountains' lofty range,
  Now left their foreheads bare,
And round the skirts their mantle furled,
Or on the sable waters curled,
Or, on the eddying breezes whirled,
  Dispersed in middle air.
And oft, condensed, at once they lower,

When, brief and fierce, the mountain shower
    Pours like a torrent down,
And when return the sun's glad beams,
Whitened with foam a thousand streams
    Leap from the mountain's crown.
[. . .]

Wester Ross

by **NAOMI MITCHISON** (1897–1999)

Published 1978

III

Stone and rock,
Boulder and pebble,
Water and stone,
Heather and stone,
Heather and water
And the bog cotton that is not for weaving.

Peats uncut
And the orange moss
Under sharp rush
And spiked deer-grass,
Under tough myrtle
And thin blue milkwort,
And ever, ever,
The silver shining
Of the bog cotton that is not flowers.

The stones drop
From the height of the bens,

In the low houses
Of the dead crofters
The rafters drop,
And the turf roof:
Stone after stone
The walls are dropping,
And the bog creeps nearer
With the bog cotton for the fairies' flag.

Born in Edinburgh and widely travelled in Asia and Africa, the 'grand dame of Scottish letters' and author of more than seventy novels (best known: *The Corn King and the Spring Queen* of 1931) moved to Carradale in Kintyre in 1939 and became deeply involved in Scottish Nationalism and local politics. Among the various committees on which Naomi Mitchison sat was the Highlands & Islands Advisory Panel, for which she composed three poems, this being the third.

A Man in Assynt

by NORMAN MACCAIG (1910–1996)

Published 1969

Glaciers, grinding West, gouged out
these valleys, rasping the brown sandstone,
and left, on the hard rock below – the
ruffled foreland –
this frieze of mountains, filed
on the blue air – Stac Polly,
Cul Beag, Cul Mor, Suilven,
Canisp – a frieze and
a litany.

Who owns this landscape?
Has owning anything to do with love?
For it and I have a love-affair, so nearly human
we even have quarrels. –
When I intrude too confidently
it rebuffs me with a wind like a hand
or puts in my way
a quaking bog or a loch
where no loch should be. Or I turn stonily
away, refusing to notice
the rouged rocks, the mascara
under a dripping ledge, even
the tossed, the stony limbs waiting.
[. . .]
Who owns this landscape? –
The millionaire who bought it or
the poacher staggering downhill in the early morning
with a deer on his back?

Who possesses this landscape? –
The man who bought it or
I who am possessed by it?

False questions, for
this landscape is
masterless
and intractable in any terms
that are human.
It is docile only to the weather
and its indefatigable lieutenants –
wind, water and frost.
The wind whets the high ridges

and stunts silver birches and alders.
Rain falling down meets
springs gushing up –
they gather and carry down to the Minch
tons of sour soil, making bald
the bony scalp of Cul Mor. And frost
thrusts his hand in cracks and, clenching his fist,
bursts open the sandstone plates,
the armour of Suilven:
he bleeds stones down chutes and screes,
smelling of gunpowder.

Or has it come to this,
that this dying landscape belongs
to the dead, the crofters and fighters
and fishermen whose larochs
sink into the bracken
by Loch Assynt and Loch Crocach? –
to men trampled under the hoofs of sheep
and driven by deer to
the ends of the earth – to men whose loyalty
was so great it accepted their own betrayal
by their own chiefs and whose descendants now
are kept in their place
by English businessmen and the indifference
of a remote and ignorant government.
[. . .]

Assynt in the north-west Highlands is a recurring theme in the poetry of Norman MacCaig, who divided his time between there and Edinburgh while working as a primary school teacher for many years. As with the artist D. Y. Cameron, whose masterpiece of subtle tonality *Wilds of Assynt* (c.1936) hangs in Perth Museum and Art Gallery, MacCaig's work resisted the nostalgic, sentimental view of the Highlands. The theme of land ownership in this poem is prescient: in 1993 the Assynt Crofters' Trust bought the northwest part of Assynt, which the Vestey family had renamed the North Lochinver Estate, and, in 2005, the community of Assynt completed the landmark buyout of 44,400 acres of the parish, comprising the Glencanisp and Drumrunie estates, formerly owned by the Vesteys.

The result of a rare commission, this is an unusual work by MacCaig, who, when asked how long it took him to write a piece, replied: 'if it's a short poem, one fag, or two if it's a long one'. *A Man in Assynt* is both his longest and only openly politically-committed work, neither of which suits his usual 'innate scepticism and talent for epigram and short lyric'. As Andrew Greig records in *At the Loch of the Green Corrie* (2010), MacCaig thought it 'not a very good poem'. Yet 'to people who live here, these are Norman MacCaig's best known and most treasured lines, cropping up again and again in people's memories, in articles, pamphlets, guidebooks…'.

Ballad of the Men of Knoydart

by **HAMISH HENDERSON** (1919–2002)

*c.*1949

'Twas down by the farm of Scottas
Lord Brocket walked one day,
And he saw a sight that worried him
Far more than he could say –
For the seven men of Knoydart
Were doing what they'd planned:

They had staked their claims and were digging their drains
On Brocket's 'Private Land!'

'You bloody red,' Lord Brocket yelled
'Wot's this you're doin' 'ere?
It doesn't pay, as you'll find today
To insult an English peer!
You're only Scottish half wits!
But I'll make you understand –
You Highland swine, these hills are mine!
This is all Lord Brocket's land.

I'll write to Arthur Woodburn's boys
And they will let you know
That the sacred rights of property
Will never be laid low;
With your stakes and tapes I'll make you traipse
From Knoydart to the Rand.
You can dig for gold till you're stiff and cold
But not on this 'ere land!'

Then up spake the men of Knoydart-
'You shut your f—ing trap!
For threats from an English brewer's boy
We just don't give a rap.
For we are all ex-servicemen,
We fought against the Hun –
We can tell our enemies by now –
And Brocket you are one!'

When he heard these words that noble peer
Turned purple in the face.
He said, 'These Scottish savages
Are Britain's black disgrace.

It may be true that I've let some few
Thousand acres go to pot,
But each one I'd give to a London spiv,
Before any Goddam Scot!'

'You're a crowd of Tartan Bolshies!
But I'll soon have you licked.
I'll write to the Court of Session,
For an Interim Interdict.
I'll write to my London lawyers,
And they will understand.'
'Och to Hell with your London lawyers,
We want our Highland Land.'

When Brocket heard these fightin' words,
He fell down in a swoon,
But they splashed his jowl with uisge,
And·he woke up mighty soon,
And he moaned, 'These Dukes of Sutherland
Were right about the Scot.
If I had my way I'd start today,
And clear the whole damn lot!'

'You may scream and yell, Lord Brocket –
You may rave and stamp and shout!
But the lamp we've lit in Knoydart
Will never now go out.
For Scotland's on the march, my boys –
We think it won't be long:
Roll on the day, when the Knoydart way
Is Scotland's Battle Song!'

This poem highlights the vicissitudes of Highland landlordism experienced by many Highland communities in recent and living memory, the undimmed consciousness of which adds an emotional intensity to the continuing debate on land reform. Still inaccessible by road, the mountain fastness of Knoydart formed part of the Lordship of Garmoran from the twelfth century and for seven hundred years belonged to different branches of the same family. Then, in 1857, having perpetrated one of the most notorious clearances four years earlier, the Macdonells of Glengarry sold this last of their ancestral properties to a Lanarkshire ironmaster. There followed a succession of incoming landlords attracted mainly by the sport, who sold off portions bit by bit; Lord Brocket, an admirer of Hitler, bought Knoydart in the early 1930s. This poem relates what happened after a group of local men approached the Department of Agriculture requesting that some land be divided into small-holdings for them. When nothing more than an acknowledgement ensued, they took dramatic action in November 1948 and staked out their claim to two farms. Although their action ultimately failed in court, Brocket sold up a few years later and Henderson's final lines were prophetic: in 1999 the community (albeit now entirely made up of incomers) played a leading role in the people's land buy-out movement and took on ownership of the Knoydart estate.

Born in Perthshire, the hard-drinking, maverick poet, song-writer and folklorist Hamish Henderson spent most of his youth in England, before joining the Highland Division in the desert, where he composed some of the best poetry of the Second World War, notably *Elegies for the Dead in Cyrenaica*. He returned to Scotland after the Second World War to explore his native country with untinted spectacles, travelling the Highlands and Islands with a taperecorder and agitating for a people's republic.

Rannoch, by Glencoe

by **T. S. ELIOT** (1888–1965)

*c.*1935

Here the crow starves, here the patient stag
Breeds for the rifle. Between the soft moor
And the soft sky, scarcely room
To leap or soar. Substance crumbles, in the thin air
Moon cold or moon hot. The road winds in
Listlessness of ancient war,
Languor of broken steel,
Clamour of confused wrong, apt
In silence. Memory is strong
Beyond the bone. Pride snapped,
Shadow of pride is long, in the long pass
No concurrence of bone.

In *A Tour in Scotland 1769*, Thomas Pennant described Rannoch Moor as ' . . . truly melancholy, almost one continued scene of dusky moors, without arable land, trees, houses, or living creatures, for numbers of miles . . . ' Eliot came here in 1935 and found the desolate moor with its starving crows silent, yet echoing with memories of violence; full of brooding menace. Broken weapons and bones recall the Massacre of Glencoe; the deer stalker's rifle anticipates more slaughter to come. The spare language emphasises the contrast of softness and harshness in a landscape where rock crumbles in heat and cold but pride remains unbroken.

Inversnaid

by **GERARD MANLEY HOPKINS** (1844–89)

1881

This darksome burn, horseback brown,
His rollrock highroad roaring down,
In coop and in comb the fleece of his foam
Flutes and low to the lake falls home.

And windpuff-bonnet of fawn-froth
Turns and twindles over the broth
Of a pool so pitchblack, fell-frowning,
It rounds and rounds Despair to drowning.

Degged with dew, dappled with dew
Are the groins of the braes that the brook treads through,
Wiry heathpacks, flitches of fern,
And the beadbonny ash that sits over the burn.

What would the world be, once bereft
Of wet and wildness? Let them be left,
O let them be left, wildness and wet;
Long live the weeds and the wilderness yet.

Hopkins spent two months in Scotland in 1881, while working as a
relief temporary curate to St Joseph's Parish in Glasgow. Already
passionate about the landscape, language and legends of Wales, the
Catholic convert Jesuit priest relished the promise of a two-day visit
to the Highlands but 'never had more than a glimpse of their skirts'.
He did, however, on 28 September, get as far as Inversnaid on the
eastern shore of Loch Lomond. The result was this joyful obser-
vation of landscape and nature, expressed with brilliant intensity
and inventiveness. We must remember that Hopkins always said
his poetry should be read aloud.

Staffa

by **JOHN KEATS** (1795–1821)

1818

Not Aladdin magian
Ever such a work began;
Not the wizard of the Dee
Ever such a dream could see;
Not St John, in Patmos' Isle,
In the passion of his toil,
When he saw the churches seven,
Golden aisl'd, built up in heaven,
Gaz'd at such a rugged wonder.
As I stood its roofing under
Lo! I saw one sleeping there,
On the marble cold and bare.
While the surges wash'd his feet,
And his garments white did beat.
Drench'd about the sombre rocks,
On his neck his well-grown locks,
Lifted dry above the main,
Were upon the curl again.
'What is this? and what art thou?'
Whisper'd I, and touch'd his brow;
'What art thou? and what is this?'
Whisper'd I, and strove to kiss
The spirit's hand, to wake his eyes;
Up he started in a trice:
'I am Lycidas,' said he,
'Fam'd in funeral minstrely!

This was architectur'd thus
By the great Oceanus! –
Here his mighty waters play
Hollow organs all the day;
Here by turns his dolphins all,
Finny palmers great and small,
Come to pay devotion due –
Each a mouth of pearls must strew.
Many a mortal of these days,
Dares to pass our sacred ways,
Dares to touch audaciously
This Cathedral of the Sea!
I have been the pontiff-priest
Where the waters never rest,
Where a fledgy sea-bird choir
Soars for ever; holy fire
I have hid from mortal man;
Proteus is my Sacristan.
But the dulled eye of mortal
Hath pass'd beyond the rocky portal;
So for ever will I leave
Such a taint, and soon unweave
All the magic of the place.'

This little known and unfinished poem was written a few days after
Keats visited Fingal's Cave in Staffa on 24 July 1818 during his
Scottish tour with Charles Brown. Having walked from Dumfries,
through Burns country and north from Glasgow to Oban, they
found the tourist boat to Staffa and Iona too expensive, and so took
a ferry to Mull. There they walked a gruelling thirty-seven miles
across very rough ground in appalling weather through the Ross of

Mull, from where they ferried to Iona to see the ruins and then boarded a boat to Staffa. The basaltic sea-cave with its Ossianic associations had been 'rediscovered' by Sir Joseph Banks in 1772, and it was fast becoming a fashionable tourist attraction: 'therefore everyone concerned with it either in this town [Oban] or the island are what you call up [well to do] . . . this irritated me', wrote Keats to his brother Tom. In this poem, which he sent with the letter, he takes inspiration from Milton and imagines encountering Lycidas, who complains of the recent violation of his solitude. Andrew Motion, in his biography of the poet, dismisses *Staffa* as 'some doggerel which uncomfortably proves his contention that "it is impossible to describe" the Cave . . . '. But Keats was to draw deeply on his profound impressions of Staffa in his great poem *Hyperion*, begun immediately on his return but never completed. As Byron observed, it 'seems actually inspired by the Titans, and is as sublime as Aeschylus'.

It is a poignant fact that the exertions of this part of the trip were to cause a grave exacerbation of the poet's failing health. As Motion says, 'It was on Mull that his short life started to end, and his slow death began'. By the time he reached Inverness on 6th August 1818, Keats had walked about 642 miles (including climbing Ben Nevis, where he sat on the edge of a precipice and composed a sonnet), and a doctor ordered him to return home immediately (he departed by boat from Cromarty). By November, his brother Tom was dead; Keats himself had less than three more years to live.

The Little White Rose

by **HUGH MACDIARMID** (1892–1978)

1934

The rose of all the world is not for me.
I want for my part
Only the little white rose of Scotland
That smells sharp and sweet – and breaks the heart.

In his first line, MacDiarmid refers directly to the opening lines of Yeats's poem *The Rose of Battle* - 'Rose of all Roses, Rose of all the World!'. For Yeats, the rose was a potent and complex symbol representing the feminine ideal; Ireland; a transcendent state of peace and beauty; ineffable perfection. But MacDiarmid rejects the universal for the particular. He wants something more specific and singular - the little white rose of Scotland, the Jacobite emblem, vulnerable yet tough. *Rosa x alba* is its correct name – 'vigorous, resistant to disease and capable of thriving on poorer soils.' For MacDiarmid, it symbolises the country he loves; for Alex Salmond, leader of the Scottish National Party, too: upbraided for wearing a Jacobite rose in his buttonhole, Salmond's retort was that it's MacDiarmid's rose and it stands for the whole of Scotland.

The White Air of March

by **IAIN CRICHTON SMITH** (1928–1998)
(Iain Mac a' Ghobhainn)

Published 1972
From a poem in 16 parts

1

This is the land God gave to Andy Stewart –
      we have our inheritance.
There shall be no ardour, there shall be indifference.
There shall not be excellence, there shall be the average.
We shall be the intrepid hunters of golf balls.

Have you not known, have you not heard, has it not been reported
that Mrs Macdonald has given an hour-long lecture on Islay
and at the conclusion was presented with a bouquet of flowers
by Marjory, aged five?
            Have you not noted
the photograph of the whist drive, skeleton hands,
rings on the skeleton fingers?
            Have you not seen
the glossy weddings in the glossy pages,
champagne and a 'shared joke'.
            Do you not see
the Music Hall's still alive here in the North? and on the stage
the yellow gorse is growing.
            'Tragedy,' said Walpole, 'for those who feel.
For those who think, it's comic'.
            Pity then those who feel
And, as for the Scottish Soldier, off to the wars!
The Cuillins stand and will forever stand.
Their streams scream in the moonlight.

2

The Cuillins tower
clear and white.
In the crevices the Gaelic bluebells flower.

(Eastward
Culloden
where the sun shone
on the feeding raven.
Let it be forgotten!)

The Cuillins tower
scale on scale.
The music of the imagination must be restored
upward.

(The little Highland dancer
in white shirt green kilt
regards her toe
arms akimbo.
Avoids the swords.)

To avoid the sword
is death.
       To walk the ward
of Dettol, loss of will,
where old men watch the wall,
eyes in a black wheel,
and the nurse in a starched dress
changes the air.

The Cuillins tower
tall and white.
March breeds white sails.

The eagle soars.
On the highest peaks
The sharpest axe.
[. . .]

15

The Cuillins tower high in the air –

Excellence.

We climb from pain to perfume:
the body opens out; gullies,
crevices, reveal the orchis.
The soul flies skyward,
impregnated with scent.
On the right hand
the sun will tenant
Skye.

The mist dissipates.

Gold grows at our feet.
[. . .]

Iain Crichton Smith wrote this poem on the theme of struggle and renewal as he was emerging from a period of deep depression. Through the collage of ephemeral images charting the decline of the modern Highlands against the symbolic backdrop of the Cuillin, the seeds of regeneration have taken root.

Canedolia: An Off-concrete Scotch Fantasia

by EDWIN MORGAN (b.1920)

Published 1982

ao! hoy! awe! ba! mey!

who saw?
rhu saw rum. garve saw smoo. nigg saw tain. lairg saw lagg.
rigg saw eigg. largs saw haggs. tongue saw luss. mull saw yell.
stoer saw strone. drem saw muck. gask saw noss. unst saw
    cults.
echt saw banff. weem saw wick. trool saw twatt.

how far?
from largo to lunga from joppa to skibo from ratho to shona
    from
ulva to minto from tinto to tolsta from soutra to marsco from
braco to barra from alva to stobo from fogo to fada from gigha
    to
gogo from kelso to stroma from hirta to spango.

what is it like there?
och it's freuchie, it's faifley, it's wamphray, it's frandy, it's
    sliddery.

what do you do?
we foindle and fungle, we bonkle and meigle and maxpoffle.
    we scotstarvit, armit, wormit, and even whifflet. we play
    at crosstobs,
leuchars, gorbals, and finfan. we scavaig, and there's aye a bit
    of
tilquhilly. if it's wet, treshnish and mishnish.

what is the best of the country?
blinkbonny! airgold! thundergay!

and the worst?
scrishven, shiskine, scrabster, and snizort.

listen! what's that?
catacol and wauchope, never heed them.

tell us about last night
well, we had a wee ferintosh and we lay on the quiraing. it was
pure strontian!

but who was there?
petermoidart and craigenkenneth and cambusputtock and
ecclemuchty and corriehulish and balladolly and altnacanny and
clauchanvrechan and stronachlochan and auchenlachar and
tighnacrankie and tilliebruaich and killieharra and invervannach and
achnatudlem and machrishellach and inchtamurchan and
auchterfechan and kinlochculter and ardnawhallie and
invershuggle.

and what was the toast?
schiehallion! schiehallion! schiehallion!

A key figure in the twentieth century renaissance of Scottish poetry,
Edwin Morgan is a fine linguist, former Professor of English at
Glasgow University and the first Scots Makar (Scottish national
poet). This poem, with its anagrammatic title, makes a play on
language and multilingualism by experimenting freely with the rich
natural poetry of Scottish place names. The result is a language that
is both confused yet curiously familiar. A fragment is engraved into
the wall of the Scottish Parliament building in Edinburgh.

LEGEND

Far-flung on the north-western extremity of Europe, the Highlands and Islands feel today like a region on the edge. But there was a time when the northern sea-lanes put Scotland at the centre of an active exchange of culture, both creative and destructive. It was here that Christianity first secured a foothold on the British mainland, and here that the Vikings extended their Danelaw in the ninth century. Many of the most stirring historic events of the Gàidhealtachd, the saints, warriors and seafarers that people Highland history, have acquired a legendary status, charged with the romance of drama and setting, reworked, mythologised and enveloped over the years by nostalgic sentimentality for the past.

Last Verse in Praise of Colum Cille

attributed to **BECCÁN MAC LUIGDECH OF RUM** (d.677)

Translated from early Gaelic by Thomas Owen Clancy

He brings northward to meet the Lord a bright crowd of chancels –
Colum Cille, kirks for hundreds, widespread candle.

Wonderful news: a realm with God after the race,
a grand kingdom, since He's set out my life's progress.

He broke passions, brought to ruin secure prisons;
Colum Cille overcame them with bright actions.

Connacht's candle, Britain's candle, splendid ruler;
in scores of curraghs with an army of wretches he crossed the long-
       haired sea.

He crossed the wave-strewn wild region, foam-flecked, seal-filled,
savage, bounding, seething, white-tipped, pleasing, doleful.

Wisdom's champion all round Ireland, he was exalted;
excellent name: Europe is nursed, Britain' sated.

Stout post, milk of meditation, with broad actions,
Colum Cille, perfect customs, fairer than trappings.

On the loud sea he cried to the King who rules thousands,
who rules the plain above cleared fields, kings and countries.

In the Trinity's care he sought a ship – good his leaving –
on high with God, who always watched him, morning, evening.

Shepherd of monks, judge of clerics, finer than things,
than kingly gates, than sounds of plagues, than battalions.

Colum Cille, candle brightening legal theory;
the race he ran pierced the midnight of Erc's region.

The skies' kind one, he tends the clouds of harsh heaven;
my soul's shelter, my poetry's fort, Conal's descendant.

Fame with virtues, a good life, his: barque of treasure,
sea of knowledge, Conal's offspring, people's counsellor.

Leafy oak-tree, soul's protection, rock of safety,
the sun of monks, mighty ruler, Colum Cille.

Beloved of God, he lived against a stringent rock,
a rough struggle, the place one could find Colum's bed.

He crucified his body, left behind sleek sides;
he chose learning, embraced stone slabs, gave up bedding.

He gave up beds, abandoned sleep, finest actions;
conquered angers, was ecstatic, sleeping little.

He possessed books, renounced fully claims of kinship:
for love of learning he gave up wars, gave up strongholds.

He left chariots, he loved ships, foe to falsehood;
sun-like exile, sailing, he left fame's steel bindings.

Colum Cille, Colum who was, Colum who will be,
constant Colum, not he a protector to be lamented.

Colum, we sing, until death's tryst, after, before,
By poetry's rules, which gives welcome to him we serve.

I pray a great prayer to Eithne's son – better than treasure –
my soul to his right hand, to heaven, before the world's people.

He worked for God, kingly prayer, within church ramparts,
with angels' will, Conal's household's child, in vestments.

Triumphant plea: adoring god, nightly, daily,
with hands outstretched, with splendid alms, with right actions.

Fine his body, Colum Cille, heaven's cleric –
a widowed crowd – well-spoken just one, tongue triumphant.

Composed some decades after St Columba's death in 597, this
poem celebrates the earthly and spiritual attributes of the Irish saint
(Colum Cille – Dove of the Church), who sailed over from Ulster
with twelve disciples in 563 and established on Iona the mother
church of Celtic Christianity in Scotland. The poem is attributed to
Beccán mac Luigdech, probably the same Beccán (a kinsman of
Columba's) who was active in Iona in the 630s and later became a
hermit scribe living on Rum. The significance of the sea to these
early Christian missionaries sequestered in their island sanctuaries
flows through the lyrical language of this beautiful poem.

Icelandic Verse

by BJORN CRIPPLEHAND

c.1100

Translated by Erling Monsen (1932)

The fire over Lewis
Played high in the heaven;
Far fled the folk;
The flame rose from the houses.

The prince went through Uist
With fire; and the bonders lost
Wealth and life; the king
Dyed his sword red in blood.

He sated the eagles' hunger
And harried far about Skye.
The glad wolf battened his teeth
In blood, on Tirey.

The maidens south in the isles
Got sorrow from the lord of Greenland.
The foe of the Scots harried,
The folk in Mull fled.

To the level Sandey the sharp
King brought the shield of war.
There was smoke over Isla, where the men
Of Magnus increased the burning.

South of Cantire the folk
Sank down beneath the swords;
The wise lord of victory
Then felled the dwellers of Man.

This early account of the Norse subjugation of the Hebrides in 1098 was composed by Bjorn Cripplehand, court-poet to Magnus Barelegs, son of Olav and King of Norway from 1093–1103. According to Snorre Sturluson (1178–1241), who included the poem in his *Heimskringla* or *The Lives of the Norse Kings* (*c.*1230), 'King Magnus went on a journey from the land; he had with him a big fine army and good ships. With this army he sailed west over the seas and came first to the Orkneys . . . [He] then sailed south with his army to the Hebrides, and when he came thither he straightway began to harry and burn the settlements; he slew the men wherever he went. The land folk fled far and wide, some to the fjords of Scotland, some south to Cantire [Kintyre] or out to Ireland. Some got quarter and submitted to him . . . King Magnus came with his army to the holy isle [Iona] and there gave quarter and peace to all men and their goods.'

The Kirk and the Ship

by GEORGE MACKAY BROWN (1921–96)

Published 1999

The master mason said
'Sail to the island of Eday
And quarry blocks of yellow stone.'

Others drove oxen to the Head of Holland
Where sandstone is red.
The lark's skein
About and about the April hill was thrown.

They did that work, the labouring Orkneymen.

Masons from Durham, strange speakers,
Squared the blocks rough-hewn.

And the Kirkwall villagers
Paused, and shook wondering heads, and went on.

And the kirk grew, like a lovely ship
Freighted with psalm and ceremony, blissward blown.

*

He that ordered the minster
Fluttered in a frailer ship
Across the Mediterranean
With pauses for dalliance, siege, piracy
But always, Jerusalem-drawn.

*

Pillars soared up, red as fire or blood.
And in one they laid
Their martyr, Magnus: his breached bellchambered bone.

George Mackay Brown's religious journey was a central theme in his life and work. Born a Presbyterian, he converted to Catholicism in 1961, and his Catholic faith enlightened his poetry and shaped his response to the history and landscape of his native Orkney. St Magnus, martyred in April 1117, was an inspirational figure for George Mackay Brown, who made him the subject of at least seven poems and of his finest novel, *Magnus* (1973). The poet died on 13 April 1996 and his funeral was held three days later, on St Magnus Day, at St Magnus Cathedral in Kirkwall. It was the first time a Catholic priest had celebrated a Requiem Mass in the cathedral since the Reformation.

Luinneag Mhic Leòid

(MacLeod's Lilt)

by **MARY MACLEOD** (*c.*1615–*c.*1707)

(Màiri nighean Alasdair Ruaidh)

Late 1600s
Translated from the Gaelic by J. Carmichael Watson, 1934

[. . .]

Thou of form so fair, without flaw of fashioning, thou heart manly
   and generous, well do red and white become thee; thy clear-
   seeing eye blue as the blueberry, set by thy cheek ruddy as the
   berry of the dog-rose.

Thy cheek is ruddy as the berry of the dog-rose, and under the
   choicest head of hair thy curling locks entwine. In thy dwelling
   would be found, ranged upon the weapon-rack, powder-horn
   and shot-horn and the choice of every armoury.

Powder-horn and shot-horn and the choice of every armoury, and
   sword-blades slender-tapering from hilt to the tip; would be
   found on each side of them rifle and carbine, and bows tough
   and sound with their bow strings of hemp.

Bows tough and sound with their bow strings of hemp, and narrow
   culverins would be bought although dear; a handful of polished
   arrows thrust down into quivers, fletched from the plumage of
   the eagle and the silk of Galway.

Fletched from the eagle's plumage and the silk of Galway; the hero
   hath my love, may Mary's Son prosper him! It would be my
   dear one's pleasure to be a-hunting in the peaks, taking joy of
   the forest and ascending the rough dells.

Taking joy of the forest and ascending the rough dells, letting slip the young hounds and inciting the old ones; of that incitement it would come that blood would flow on the bristles of the folk of white flanks and russet mantles.

Blood on the deer white-flanked and russet-mantled, at the hands of thy company of nobles that bear hardly on their weapons; men that well would read the day, and speed over the ocean, and fit to sail the vessel to the haven wherein she would be beached.

[. . .]

This song is among the best known by Mary MacLeod, the famous bardess who, with Iain Lom (John Macdonald), was a leading figure in the seventeeth century renaissance of Gaelic poetry. Born at Rodel in Harris and appointed nurse at Dunvegan Castle, she was later banished for something she did or composed and made this song while in exile, probably on Scarba. She was later recalled and lived to be over one hundred, always carrying her whisky, snuff and a silver-headed staff.

The Bardess of Dunvegan stood at a watershed, when the formal literary language of the old bards began to be replaced by the Gaelic vernacular. She assimilated traditional elements into a new, popular style of poetry, composing rhythmic, song-like pieces with a richness of assonance and idiom that appealed principally to the heart and the ear.

Luinneag Mhic Leòid echoes the courtly panegyric tradition of bardic praise to a chief, although its flow is more spontaneous and its diction and versification are in the popular style. Despite the title, its subject, the romantic Royalist military hero Sir Norman MacLeod of Bernera (1614–1705), was not a chief and would not therefore have been known as 'MacLeod'. He was, however, a generous patron of bards, musicians and story tellers and many of Mary's songs are addressed to him. They convey her delight in manly vigour and beauty, sporting and military prowess, singing and music.

The Birlinn of Clanranald
(Birlinn Chlann Raghnaill)

by **ALEXANDER MACDONALD** (c.1698–c.1770)
(Alasdair Mac Mhaighstir Alasdair)

Written after 1751; first published 1776
Translated from the Gaelic by Hugh MacDiarmid, 1935

[. . .]
Incitement for Rowing to Sailing-Place

To put the black well-fashioned yewship
    To the sailing-place
Thrust you out flexible oarbanks
    Dressed to sheer grace;
Oars smooth-shafted and shapely,
    Grateful for gripping,
Made for lusty resolute rowing,
    Palm-fast, foam-whipping;
Knocking sparks out of the water
    Towards Heaven
Like the fire-flush from a smithy
    Updriven,
Under the great measured onstrokes
    Of the oar-lunges
That confound the indrawn billows
    With their plunges,
While the shrewd blades of the white woods
    Go cleaving

The tops of the valleyed blue-hills
    Shaggily heaving.
O stretch you, pull you, and bend you
    Between the thole-pins,
Your knuckles snow with hard plying
    The pinewood fins;
All the big muscular fellows
    Along her lying
With their hairy and sinewy
    Arms keep her flying,
Raising and lowering together
    With a single motion
Their evenly dressed poles of pinewood
    Mastering the ocean.

A Herculean planked on the fore-oar
    Roaring: 'Up, on with her!'
Makes all the thick shoulder muscles
    Glide better together,
Thrusting the birlinn with snorting
    Through each chill sea-glen;
The hard curved prow through the tide-lumps
    Drives inveighing,
On all hands sending up mountains
    Round her insistence.
[. . .]

The Voyage
[. . .]
Then opened the windows of the sky
    Pied, grey-blue,
To the lowering wind's blowing,
    A morose brew,

The sea pulled on his grim rugging
  Slashed with sore rents,
That rough-napped mantle, a weaving
  Of loathsome torrents.
The shape-ever-changing surges
  Swelled up in hills
And roared down into valleys
  In appalling spills.
The water yawned in great craters,
  Slavering mouths agape
Snatching and snarling at each other
  In rabid shape.
It were a man's deed to confront
  The demented scene,
Each mountain of them breaking
  Into flamy lumps.
Each fore-wave towering grey-fanged
  Mordantly grumps
While a routing comes from the black-waves
  With their raving rumps.
When we would rise on these rollers
  Soundly, compactly,
It was imperative to shorten sail
  Swiftly, exactly.
When we would fall with no swallowing
  Down into the glens
Every topsail she had would be off.
  – No light task the men's!
The great hooked big-buttocked ones
  Long before
They came at all near us were heard
  Loudly aroar

Scourging all the lesser waves level
    As on they tore.
It was no joke to steer in that sea
    When the high tops to miss
Seemed almost to hear her keel scrape
    The shelly abyss!
The sea churning and lashing itself
    In maniacal states,
[. . .]
– But when it was beyond the sea's power
    To make us yield
She took pity with a faint smile
    And truce was sealed,
Though by that time no mast was unbent,
    No sail untorn,
Yard unsevered, mast-ring unflawed,
    Oar not shag-shorn,
No stay unstarted, halyard or shroud unbroken.
[. . .]

The sea journey of Clanranald's *birlinn* (galley) is a sublime master-piece of Gaelic poetry by the brilliant and inventive Alexander Macdonald. Extending to more than 600 lines divided into 16 parts, the Homeric epic is an eighteenth century variation on the great voyage poetry of the Gaelic bards, a sea odyssey described with words of awesome power. The poem opens with a traditional ship's blessing and blessing of arms, followed by an incitement to row to the sailing place and a rowing song. The crew is then deployed and the galley sets out on St Brigid's day to sail from Loch Eynort in South Uist to Carrickfergus in Antrim. She survives a terrible storm and eventually, after the crew has offered thanks to the High King, arrives safely in Ireland. The poem echoes the traditional panegyric rhetoric of bardic verse, but here, although the chief is praised several times, the main focus of attention is the crew. It can be interpretated as an allegory on the Forty-Five, in which the oarsmen – the ordinary clansmen – are the heroes who must suffer for the cause.

Hugh MacDiarmid regretted not being fluent in Gaelic, which he thought was fundamental to Scotland's literary and cultural identity. He made this translation with the help of Sorley MacLean.

Pibroch Voices

by CHARLES RICHARD CAMMELL

*c.*1933

Thou art stealing, stealing the heart of me, Pibroch;
Wounding, wounding me with the wild voice of thee:
Voice of the mountain, voice of moorland and sea-waste,
Voice of the Isles, captured and chained by MacCrimmon.

Nature's voice heard by them, chiefs among pipers:
Caught and held fast by them, set here forever,
The sea-voice and hill-voice and moor-voice of Scotland,
In the pibrochs of Skye on the pipes of MacCrimmon.

Wound! Wound! How bitter are the stabs of thee,
Deep, deep, to the heart of me, sword of the Pibroch.
Gathered are the tears in thee; all the sad years in thee:
All the wounds and the woes in the voice of MacCrimmon.

There's a new note in thee; is it man or fay?
Is it God's voice in thee, crying to me, Pibroch?
Past all the pain of thee, through the refrain of thee,
Hope! The last strain on the pipes of MacCrimmon!

'The great, bellowing bagpipe that outshone every sort of music when it was played by Patrick's fingers' goes Mary MacLeod's song to Pàdraig Mór MacCrimmon (*c.*1595–1670), scion of the great Skye family of hereditary pipers to the chiefs of MacLeod. It was the MacCrimmons who developed the the classical music of the bagpipe – *ceòl mór* (the Great Music), also known as *píobaireachd* (pibroch, meaning piping) – a traditional form of music which ranks among the greatest of Scotland's artistic achievements. Intense and haunting, the pibroch is considered far superior to the more popular kinds of bagpipe music, such as marches, reels and strathspeys. The first of the MacCrimmon pipers was Iain Odhar, who is said to have received the gift of a silver chanter from a fairy one night during a full moon. The MacCrimmons were at the height of their fame in the late seventeenth century, when, in exchange for their hereditary piping duties, they lived free of all feudal impositions. Two of their pipes are preserved at Dunvegan Castle.

The shipbuilding heir Charles Cammell, a champion fencer and member of the Edinburgh literati, moved to London in 1935 and devoted himself to poetry. This poem, which celebrates the spellbinding beauty of the MacCrimmons' art, was composed by him to mark the unveiling of the monument beside the ruins of the MacCrimmons' piping college at Borreraig in Skye, which operated into the 1770s.

The Ballad of Glencoe

by JIM McLEAN

1963

Oh, cruel was the snow that sweeps Glen Coe
And covers the grave o' Donald
Oh, cruel was the foe that raped Glen Coe
And murdered the house of MacDonald

They came in a blizzard, we offered them heat
A roof for their heads, dry shoes for their feet
We wined them and dined them, they ate of our meat
And they slept in the house of MacDonald
Oh, cruel was the snow that sweeps Glen Coe
And covers the grave o' Donald
Oh, cruel was the foe that raped Glen Coe
And murdered the house of MacDonald

They came from Fort William with murder in mind
The Campbell had orders King William had signed
'Put all to the sword' – these words underlined
'And leave none alive called MacDonald'
Oh, cruel was the snow that sweeps Glen Coe
And covers the grave o' Donald
Oh, cruel was the foe that raped Glen Coe
And murdered the house of MacDonald

They came in the night when the men were asleep
This band of Argyles, through snow soft and deep
Like murdering foxes amongst helpless sheep
They slaughtered the house of MacDonald

Oh, cruel was the snow that sweeps Glen Coe
And covers the grave o' Donald
Oh, cruel was the foe that raped Glen Coe
And murdered the house of MacDonald

Some died in their beds at the hand of the foe
Some fled in the night and were lost in the snow
Some lived to accuse him who struck the first blow
But gone was the house of MacDonald
Oh, cruel was the snow that sweeps Glen Coe
And covers the grave o' Donald
Oh, cruel was the foe that raped Glen Coe
And murdered the house of MacDonald

There can be few more gruesome episodes in Highland history than the infamous Massacre of Glencoe. It was the culmination of a long chain of events generated by the uneasy relationship between Highlanders and government and the conflicting allegiances of different clans, and it represents the ultimate betrayal of the time-honored tradition of Highland hospitality. The massacre took place in the early hours of 13 February 1692, when a company of the Earl of Argyll's Regiment of Foot commanded by Captain Robert Campbell of Glenlyon carried out the order to 'fall upon the rebels the Macdonalds of Glencoe, and putt all to the sword under seventy'. The soldiers had been billeted in Glencoe for nearly two weeks, accepting generous hospitality from their Macdonald hosts, principally Alastair Macdonald ('MacIain'), chief of the Macdonalds of Glencoe and a relation of Campbell by marriage. He and thirty-seven of his clansmen were murdered and many others escaped only to perish later in the snow, bringing the final deathtoll to well over one hundred. The massacre was carried out in retribution for the chief's failure to sign his allegiance to William III by the deadline of 31 December 1691. MacIain's delay in turning up to honour this oath was the result of a cunning ruse devised by John Dalrymple, Master of Stair, at whose instigation William III gave the order to carry out the killings.

There are many songs about the Glencoe Massacre, perhaps the best-known being John MacDonald (Iain Lom) of Keppoch's *Òran Murt Ghlinne Comhann*, composed soon after the event. It is a testament to the qualities of this one that over the years the tune and words written by Jim McLean in 1963 have come to be thought of as a traditional song.

Skye Boat Song

by SIR HAROLD BOULTON (1859–1935)

1884

> *Speed bonnie boat like a bird on the wing,*
> *'Onward' the sailors cry;*
> *Carry the lad that's born to be king*
> *Over the sea to Skye.*

Loud the winds howl, loud the waves roar,
Thunderclaps rend the air;
Baffled our foes stand by the shore,
Follow they will not dare.
Chorus

Though the waves leap, soft shall ye sleep,
Ocean's a royal bed.
Rocked in the deep Flora will keep
Watch by your weary head.
Chorus

Many's the lad fought on that day
Well the claymore could wield
When the night came silently lay
Dead on Culloden's field.
Chorus

Burned are our homes, exile and death
Scatter the loyal men;
Yet, ere the sword cool in the sheath,
Charlie will come again.
Chorus

Harold Boulton, Oxford-educated son of an English chemical manufacturer, developed a passion for Scottish folk songs after an undergraduate reading party in Scotland. Enthused by Jacobite sentiment, the future director of the Royal Academy of Music travelled widely through the Highlands collecting traditional melodies, for which he wrote new songs. This, his most famous, was published in *Songs of the North* (1884), which he edited with Miss Annie Macleod (Lady Wilson) – 'a collection that every singer will desire to have, and every Scotchman will be wise to get'. The air was composed by Miss Macleod around a Gaelic rowing song heard during a trip to Skye in the 1870s. Boulton first heard it, sung to different words, while staying at Roshven in Moidart in 1882. Several days later, rattling across Germany to Cologne, 'I could not get to sleep in the train because of the lilt of the Highland Boat Song and . . . the words of the *Skye Boat Song* were forced upon me and fastened themselves on to the all-compelling tune'.

They tell the story of Bonnie Prince Charlie's escape from Benbecula, where he was hiding in the early summer of 1746, to Trotternish in Skye. He had spent several weeks skulking in a remote Uist glen, enjoying hunting and convivial drinking sessions as government men-o'-war patrolled the coast and redcoats homed in, and the noose had begun to tighten. Flora Macdonald was brought to meet him in her brother's shieling and a plan was hatched. Soon, news came that General Campbell had landed with 1,500 troops and that Captain Fergussone was approaching with another party. The prince, assuming the disguise of Flora's Irish maid, Betty Burke, put on a white and blue-sprigged 'calico gown and quilted petticoat and a mantle of dull camlet made after the Irish fashion, with a cap to cover his whole head and face' and, after darkness had fallen, embarked with Flora into the 'small shallop of about nine cubits', to be rowed over the sea to Skye.

The Eve of Waterloo

by GEORGE GORDON, LORD BYRON (1788–1824)

From *Childe Harold's Pilgrimage*, Canto III

Published 1812–18

[. . .]
And wild and high the 'Camerons' Gathering' rose!
The war-note of Lochiel, which Albyn's hills
Have heard, and heard, too, have her Saxon foes:-
How in the noon of night that Pibroch thrills,
Savage and shrill! But with the breath which fills
Their mountain-pipe, so fill their mountaineers
With the fierce native daring which instils
The stirring memory of a thousand years,
And Evan's, Donald's fame rings in each clansman's ears!
[. . .]

On the night of 15 June 1815, the Duchess of Richmond gave a ball in Brussels, to which many of the officers of the allied English and Prussian armies were invited. During the evening, a messenger brought word to the Duke of Wellington, commander-in-chief of the British Army, that Napoleon's troops were advancing on the city. Not wishing to alarm the guests, Wellington told his officers to depart discreetly to join their regiments and finally left the ball himself. Soon, a distant booming was heard and, although at first the guests paid little attention and carried on dancing, the cannons' roar came nearer. This stanza describes the 79th or Cameron Highlanders, the regiment raised by Sir Alan Cameron of Erracht in 1793, marching out of the city at sunrise to secure the crossroads at Quatre Bras two days before the Battle of Waterloo. It emphasises the changing attitude to Highlanders after the clan system was dismantled in the eighteenth century. Previously regarded as unruly and rebellious, they were now celebrated for their warlike spirit and loyalty as soldiers in the British army. Only the Highland regiments were exempt from the ban on Highland dress and arms, and thus they assumed a glamour and image of romantic heroism that played a significant role in the promotion of tartan as a national symbol.

LOSS

The revolutionary potential of poetry, its capacity for indignation, often using potent symbolism, comes to the fore in this selection of poems. Themes of dispossession, lamentation and longing recur. Many address the involuntary losses suffered by Highlanders and Hebrideans as a result of the Jacobite uprisings of 1715 and 1745, and the forced evictions and exile imposed by the Clearances.

The Bonnie Banks o' Loch Lomond

By yon bonnie banks and by yon bonnie braes,
Where the sun shines bright on Loch Lomond,
Where me and my true love were ever wont to gae,
On the bonnie, bonnie banks o' Loch Lomond.

Chorus
O ye'll tak' the high road and I'll tak' the low road,
And I'll be in Scotland afore ye,
But me and my true love will never meet again
On the bonnie, bonnie banks o' Loch Lomond.

'Twas there that we parted in yon shady glen,
On the steep, steep side o' Ben Lomond,
Where in purple hue the Hieland hills we view,
And the moon coming out in the gloamin'.
Chorus

The wee birdies sing and the wild flowers spring,
And in sunshine the waters are sleepin';
But the broken heart it kens nae second spring again
Though the waefu' may cease from their greetin'.
Chorus

Everybody knows this song, but few the origin of the words, which
are not so much about Loch Lomond as love, death and loss. One
interpretation of the road theme alludes to the belief in a spiritual
'low road' on which the dead journey faster than the living, who
must take the 'high road' over physical terrain. The 'you' and 'I' in
the song are said to be two soldiers captured after the Forty-Five.
One is to be released – he will take the high road home over the
Cheviots. The other is to be executed and will never see his love
again, even though his spirit will reach home first by the low road.

Will Ye No Come Back Again?

Bonnie Charlie's now awa',
Safely o'er the friendly main,
Mony a heart will break in twa,
Should he ne'er come back again.

Will ye no come back again?
Will ye no come back again?
Better lo'ed ye canna be
Will ye no come back again

Ye trusted in your Hieland men,
They trusted you dear Charlie!
They kent your hiding in the glen,
Death and exile braving.

Will ye no come back again? Etc

English bribes were a' in vain,
Tho' puir and puirer we maun be;
Siller canna buy the heart,
That aye beats warm for thine and thee.

Will ye no come back again? Etc

We watch'd thee in the gloamin' hour;
We watch'd thee in the mornin' grey;
Tho' thirty thousand pounds they gi'e,
Oh, there is nane that wad betray!

Will ye no come back again? Etc

Sweet's the laverock's note and lang,
Liltin' wildly up the glen;

But aye to me he sings ae sang,
'Will ye no come back again?'

Will ye no come back again? Etc

James Hogg recorded slightly different words (he didn't identify his source) and other versions are said to have been in circulation, but the song as reproduced here is attributed to Carolina Oliphant, Lady Nairne (1766–1845), a great admirer of Burns who composed her own words to traditional airs. The symbolic use of birds (as in the laverock (skylark) here) was a familiar device in Jacobite laments.

The Proud Plaid

by ALEXANDER MACDONALD (*c*.1698–*c*.1770)

(Alasdair Mac Mhaighstir Alasdair)

c.1747

Translated from the Gaelic by John Lorne Campbell c.1930

[. . .]
True dress of the soldier,
Practical, when sounds the war-cry,
Graceful in the advance thou art,
When bagpipes sound and banners flutter.

Thou'rt splendid too, when comes the charge,
And swords are drawn from scabbards,
The finest garb to set the rout,
And in the feet put swiftness.

Thou wast good to hunt the deer in,
When the sun arose o'er the hillside,

And I would lightly go in thee
Sunday morning churchwards.

Closely wrapped I'd lie in thee,
And like the roedeer spring up quickly,
Far readier to wield my arms
Than red coat with his clattering musket.

When the black-cock's murmuring
On a knoll in th' dewy morning,
'Twas finer then to use thee
Than any dirty ragged black coat.

In thee I'd go to weddings,
And never brush the dewy grass,
That was the handsome garment
That dearly loved the bride to see.

In woodlands thou wast splendid
To give me covering and warmth,
From driven snow or Scots mist
Or showers thou wast my guard.

Above thee, truly beautiful,
Would lie the carved shield,
And the sword, on handsome belt,
Aslant thy pleated folds.

Well with thee would go my gun
Lightly beneath my arm,
Thou wast my full protection
From rain and storm and every ill.

Thou wast fine at night time,
My choice thou wast as bed-clothes;

Better than the finest sheets
Of costly linen in Glasgow.
[. . .]
Thou'rt good by day or night time,
And comely upon hill or sea-shore,
In hosting or in peace time,
No King was he who thee forbade.

He thought that thus he'd blunted
The keenness of the Gaels so valiant,
But he has only made them
Still sharper than the edge of razor.

He's left them full of malice,
As ravenous as dogs a-starving,
No draught can quench their thirst now
Of any wine, save England's life-blood.

Though you tear our hearts out,
And rend apart our bosoms,
Never shall you take Prince Charles
From us, till we're a-dying.

To our souls he's woven,
Firmly waulked, and tightly locked,
Ne'er can he be loosened
From us till he is cut away.

Just as the wife in travail
Suffers ere her child's delivered,
Yet instead of turning from him,
Her passion for her spouse is doubled.

Though on us you've put fetters
Tightly-fixed to stop us moving,

Yet will we run as swiftly,
More tireless than the deer on hillside.

We're still of our old nature
As were we ere the Act was passed,
Alike in mind and persons
And loyalty, we will not weaken.

Our blood is still our fathers',
And ours the valour of their hearts,
The inheritance they left us
Loyalty – that is our creed.

Cursed be every person
Who's still unwilling to rise for thee
Whether he has clothing,
Or though he be stark naked.

My darling the young hero,
Who left us to go o'er the sea,
Thy country's warmest wishes
And prayers will follow thee.

A luminary among eighteenth-century Gaelic poets, the rugged and impetuous Alexander Macdonald (son of the Episcopalian clergyman *Maighstir Alasdair,* and first cousin of Flora Macdonald) converted to Catholicism and gradually reverted to his early Jacobite allegiance between 1729 and 1745, while working as a Presbyterian schoolmaster and catechist in Ardnamurchan. The poet was actively engaged in the Forty-Five Rising and among the first to greet Bonnie Prince Charlie when he sailed into Loch nan Uamh in July 1745. Among the pieces published in his collection *Ais-Eiridh na Sean Chánoin Albannaich* (The Resurrection of the Ancient Scottish

Language) in 1751 were some of the most passionately patriotic (and seditious) Gaelic poems ever written.

This one was ignited by fury over the Act for Abolition and Proscription of the Highland Dress, which, following on from the disarming act of 1716, was imposed by the government in 1747 as part of its bid to dismantle all elements of Highland culture and thereby forestall further insurrection. The penalty for disobeying was six months' imprisonment for the first offence, seven years' transportation for the second. The Act not only dealt a cruel blow to Highland pride; it also forced many in remote areas who could not obtain Lowland garments to wear ludicrous outfits in order to comply. In 1782, largely due to the efforts of the Highland Society of London and its then president, the Marquess of Graham, the Acts were repealed.

A note in *Highlanders of Scotland* describes the traditional Highland garb as: ' . . . a saffron *leine* or shirt, a plaid [from the Gaelic *plaide* – a blanket or length of woollen cloth] thrown over the shoulders, and brought to the knees all round in plaits and also belted, a bonnet (sometimes) and brogues made of skin, sometimes with hose; knees always bare . . . The modern kilt [*philabeg*] is merely the lower half of the *breacan* or feile (the plaid) cut off from the upper, a jacket being made of the upper.'

My Heart's in the Highlands

by **ROBERT BURNS** (1759–96)

1789

Farewell to the Highlands, farewell to the North,
The birthplace of valour, the country of worth;
Wherever I wander, wherever I rove,
The hills of the Highlands for ever I love.

My heart's in the Highlands, my heart is not here;
My heart's in the Highlands, a-chasing the deer;
A-chasing the wild deer, and following the roe,
My heart's in the Highlands wherever I go.

Farewell to the mountains high cover'd with snow
Farewell to the straths and green valleys below:
Farewell to the forests and wild-hanging woods;
Farewell to the torrents and loud-pouring floods.
Chorus

'My journey thro' the Highlands was perfectly inspiring; and I hope I have laid in a new stock of poetical ideas' wrote Burns after a tour of the Highlands with William Nicol in 1787. This nostalgic song describes the yearning felt by an emigrant for his native land. The first verse is from old fragments, the rest was composed by the Bard to fit an existing melody. It was published in James Johnson's *The Scots Musical Museum* (1790). Horatio McCulloch's painting, *The Emigrant's Dream of his Highland Home* (1860) was renamed *My Heart's in the Highlands* after it was engraved as an illustration to this song.

The Clearances

by **IAIN CRICHTON SMITH** (1928–1998)

(Iain Mac a' Ghobhainn)

Published 1965

The thistles climb the thatch. Forever
this sharp scale in our poems,
as also the waste music of the sea.

The stars shine over Sutherland
in a cold ceilidh of their own,
as, in the morning, the silver cane

cropped among corn. We will remember this.
Though hate is evil we cannot
but hope your courtier's heels in hell

are burning: that to hear
the thatch sizzling in tanged smoke
your hot ears slowly learn.

All over the Highlands and Islands, silent ruins bear testimony to one of the most notorious episodes in Highland history – the Clearances. During the nineteenth century, landlords seeking to eradicate over-crowding and put their land to more profitable use forcibly evicted Highlanders from their homes and had thousands shipped off to America, so that they could turn the emptied hills and glens into single sheep farms or sporting estates. Iain Crichton Smith, brought up in Lewis, was among the Gaelic speaking poets of his generation who wrote most emotively about the Clearances and the desolation that ensued. His acclaimed first novel, *Consider the Lilies* (1968), portrays the life of an old woman forced from her croft and betrayed by the church during this period of destitution and loss. Particularly notorious were the evictions in Sutherland, where this poem is set.

Hallaig

by **SORLEY MACLEAN** (1911–96)
(Somhairle MacGill-Eain)
1954
Translated from the Gaelic by the poet

'Time, the deer, is in the Wood of Hallaig.'

The window is nailed and boarded
through which I saw the West
and my love is at the Burn of Hallaig
a birch tree, and she has always been

between Inver and Milk Hollow,
here and there about Baile-chuirn:
she is a birch, a hazel,
a straight slender young rowan.

In Screapadal of my people,
where Norman and Big Hector were,
their daughters and their sons are a wood
going up beside the stream.

Proud tonight the pine cocks
crowing on the top of Cnoc an Ra
straight their backs in the moonlight-
they are not the wood I love.

I will wait for the birch wood
until it comes up by the Cairn,
until the whole ridge from Beinn na Lice
will be under its shade.

If it does not, I will go down to Hallaig,
to the Sabbath of the dead,
where the people are frequenting,
every single generation gone.

They are still in Hallaig,
Macleans and MacLeods,
all who were there in the time of MacGille Chaluim:
the dead have been seen alive –

The men lying on the green
at the end of every house that was,
the girls a wood of birches,
straight their backs, bent their heads.

Between the Leac and Fearns
the road is under mild moss
and the girls in silent bands
go to Clachan as in the beginning.

And return from Clachan,
from Suisnish and the land of the living;
each one young and light-stepping,
without the heartbreak of the tale.

From the Burn of Fearns to the raised beach
that is clear in the mystery of the hills,
there is only the congregation of the girls
keeping up the endless walk,

Coming back to Hallaig in the evening,
in the dumb living twilight,
filling the steep slopes,
their laughter in my ears a mist,

and their beauty a film on my heart
before the dimness comes on the kyles,
and when the sun goes down behind Dun Cana
a vehement bullet will come from the gun of Love;

and will strike the deer that goes dizzily,
sniffing at the grass-grown ruined homes;
his eye will freeze in the wood;
his blood will not be traced while I live.

Sorley MacLean's haunting evocation of a cleared township conveys with astonishing, hallucinatory power 'the Highland paradox of sensing both absence and continuity in the physical landscape.' Hallaig is a real place – a deserted township on the isle of Raasay, where the poet was brought up. In 1833, 'no less than 60 scholars' resided here, but Hallaig was cleared in June 1854 and used as a sheeprun, and by 1891, as the Census records, its population was 'nil'. A central theme, symbolised by the deer, is time, which has destroyed Hallaig, but which in turn is killed, bringing together the two worlds of the living and the dead. The trees of Hallaig wood are the ghosts of the past, the root and branches of MacLean's own genealogy. The poet spent his working life as a schoolmaster in Edinburgh and Plockton, after which he settled in Skye, where he lived at Braes looking out across the Sound to the woods of Raasay.

MacLean was determined to attempt nothing more in his translations than a 'faithful account of the meaning in an almost word-for-word way . . . ' He wanted Gaelic poetry to stand alone on its own merits and destroyed his early writings in English 'for patriotic reasons'. 'I could hardly bear to think of a time when there was no one left with Gaelic enough to hear to the full the great song-poetry of our people', he wrote. In retrospect, it is ironic that a poem such as *Hallaig,* which laments and reinvokes a passing civilisation, should have contributed so significantly to the renaissance of Gaelic poetry that flowered under Sorley MacLean.

The Canadian Boat Song

Listen to me, as when ye heard our father
Sing long ago the song of other shores;
Listen to me, and then in chorus gather
All your deep voices as ye pull your oars!

Fair these broad meads, these hoary woods are grand;
But we are exiles from our fathers' land.

From the lone shieling and the misty island
Mountains divide us, and a waste of seas –
Yet still the blood is strong, the heart is Highland,
And we in dreams behold the Hebrides.
Chorus

We ne'er shall tread the fancy-haunted valley,
Where 'tween the dark hills creeps the small, clear stream,
In arms around the patiarch banner rally,
Nor see the moon on royal tombstones gleam.
Chorus

When the bold kindred, in the time long-vanished,
Conquered the soil and fortified the keep,
No seer foretold the children would be banished,
That a degenerate Lord might boast his sheep.
Chorus

Come foreign rage – let discord burst in slaughter!
O then for clansmen true, and stern claymore;
The hearts that would have given their blood like water
Beat heavily beyond the Atlantic roar.
Chorus

Published in *Blackwood's Magazine* in 1829, this song has been the subject of much speculation as to its authorship. In *The Lone Shieling* (1908), G. M. Fraser of Aberdeen argued that it was certainly not 'from the Gaelic', but had probably been composed by Christopher North (pen name of John Wilson), who edited a monthly article called *Noctes Ambrosianae*. Fraser noted that it is in the style of others by him and could have been inspired by a letter North received from a friend in Canada describing being rowed down the St Lawrence river by some 'strapping fellows all born in that country and yet hardly one could speak a word of any tongue but the Gaelic. They sang heaps of our old Highland oar songs, he says, in the Hebridean fashion. He has sent me a translation of one of their ditties'.

An Ataireachd Àrd

(The Sea's Lofty Roar)

by **DONALD MACIVER** (1857–1935)
(Dòmhnall MacÌomhair)
1905
Translated from the Gaelic by Ronald Black

Endless surge of the sea,
Hear the sound of the sea's lofty roar,
The thundering swell
That I heard as a child long ago –
Without change or compassion
Dragging the sand of the shore:
Endless surge of the sea,
Hear the sound of the sea's lofty roar.

All the waves crashing down
Are trembling, loud-sounding and white,
So hurried and cruel,
Grim and spuming without taking fright;
But their speed falls away
At the same destination each time
As the people have perished
Who once dwelt in this village of mine.

In the forests of the west
I've never wanted to stay,
My mind and ambition
Set firm on the hollow of the bay;
But those who were generous
In effort, in friendship and fame
Are scattered defenceless
Like birds in their enemy's way.

Rushes and willow,
And thistle, and marram and grass,
Have choked up the springs
Where I'd find many thirst-quenching draughts;
The ruins are so cold,
With ragwort and dockens growing high,
While the red nettle swarms
Where warm is the ghost of the hearth.

But I've seen an age
When the place was both snug and alive,
With youngsters unbowed
Whose manner was proud but polite,
Their mothers serene
Well pleased with their partners in life

With sheep and with cows
Setting out at the morning's first light.

But looking around
My spirits are bound to be low:
I don't see the tenants
Whose warm generosity flowed –
As exiles in misery
They've been driven away from our shores
And they'll never now hear
The great sound of the sea's lofty roar.
[. . .]

The inspiration for this haunting emigrant song was an occasion in about 1888 when Donald MacIver, a Lewis schoolmaster, stood with his uncle watching the Atlantic breakers rolling in to the Tràigh Mhór at Carnish. His uncle was revisiting Lewis, having emigrated to Quebec in 1852, when Carnish was cleared. 'Nothing here is as it was except the surge of the sea on the strand' he said. MacIver's song, which won the 1905 National Mod poetry competition, was subsequently set to John MacDonald's beautiful slow melody. 'It crystallises, by the skilful blending of the idea of human desolation and a mournful sound in nature, a mood of universal sadness, a sense of the transience of the world . . . ' wrote Sorley MacLean.

Moladh Uibhist

(In Praise of Uist)

Translated from the Gaelic by Margaret Fay Shaw

O my country, I think of thee, fragrant, fresh Uist of the
    handsome youths, where nobles might be seen, where
    Clan Ranald had his heritage.

Land of bent grass, land of barley, land where everything is
    plentiful, where young men sing songs and drink ale.

They come to us, deceitful and cunning, in order to entice us
    from our homes; they praise Manitoba to us, a cold
    country without coal or peat.

I need not trouble to tell you it; when one arrives there one
    can see – a short summer, a peaceful autumn, and long
    winter of bad weather.

If I had as much as two suits of clothes, a pair of shoes and
    my fare in my pocket, I would sail for Uist.

This emigrant song, sung to a traditional tune, was recorded by
Margaret Fay Shaw (1903–2004) in her widely acclaimed *Folksongs
& Folklore of South Uist* (1955). Like other songs she recorded in
this book, she first heard it sung in the kitchen of Boisdale House,
South Uist by the sisters Peigi and Mairi MacRae, with whom she
lived intermittently from 1929 to 1935, and their cousin Angus
MacCuish. The words were composed by Allan MacPhee. Today
the song is probably best known as *O Mo Dhùthaich,* sung by Karen
Matheson of the band Capercaillie, in whose album *Sidewaulk* it
featured in 1993.

St Columba's Isle, Loch Erisort, Lewis

by **DERICK THOMSON** (b.1921)
(Ruaraidh MacThòmais)

*c.*1955
Translated from the Gaelic by the poet

Deserted in the noon-time's shimmering, pouring sun,
your hillsides stained with heather and with fern,
the moss and peat-mould of your glen, your meadow grass,
the rich bright field and corn-yard of the saints.

The nettles multiply beside your rain-washed stones,
showering their autumn seeds over the slabs;
where once upstanding lads joined in the song,
the never-bending iris now grows tall.

The grunting sheep have drowned the chanted psalms
long since; the fiddle's still, broken its bow;
the *Brown Mare's* fodder eaten by the winds,
and Murchadh Mòr* a cipher in his kist.

The orchard starved, the green field fallow now,
a re-created desert in God's place,
you were the seagull's land when time began,
and still the seagull hangs from its own wings.

---

* Seeing porpoises swimming in the loch, Thomson was reminded of a
poem by the seventeenth century poet, seafarer and Seaforth factor
Murdoch Mackenzie (Murchadh Mòr), who named the poem after his
boat, *An Làir Dhonn* (the Brown Mare). In it, Mackenzie contrasts his boat
with a mare, saying that it needed no chaff, or straw or mash, only the
clash of the waves on its prow.

Derick Thomson, son of poet James Thomson and raised in Lewis, was Professor of Celtic at Glasgow University from 1963 to 1991. The father of modern Gaelic publishing, he has initiated many Gaelic projects and published seven collections of his own poems. This one was written after a visit one clammy summer's afternoon in 1955 to Loch Erisort's island sanctuary, with its chapel of eighth-century origin, monastic ruins and burial ground for the dead of the neighbouring districts of Lewis.

Niel Gow's Farewell to Whisky

You've surely heard o' famous Niel,
The man that play'd the fiddle weel;
I wat he was a canty chiel,
And dearly lo'ed the whisky O.
And aye sin he wore tartan trews,
He dearly lo'ed the Athol brose;*
And wae was he, you may suppose,
To play farewell to whisky O.

Alake, quoth Niel, I'm frail and auld,
And find my bluid grow unco cauld;
I think 'twad make me blithe and bauld,
A wee drap Highland whisky O.
Yet the doctors they do a' agree,
That whisky's no the drink for me.
By Saul! quoth Niel, 'twill spoil my glee,
Should they part me and whisky O.

* Athol Brose is a drink made by mixing oatmeal brose with honey and
  whisky, and often also with cream added to make it richer, thicker and
  similar to Cranachan.

Though I can baith get wine and ale,
And find my head and fingers hale,
I'll be content, though legs should fail,
To play farewell to whisky O.
But still I think on auld lang syne,
When Paradise our friends did tyne,
Because something ran in their mind,
Forbid like Highland whisky O.

Come, a' ye powers o' music, come;
I find my heart grows unco glum;
My fiddle-string will no play bum,
To say farewell to whisky O.
Yet I'll take my fiddle in my hand,
And screw the pegs up while they'll stand,
To make a lamentation grand
For gude auld Highland whisky O.

The Perthshire fiddler and composer Niel Gow (1727–1807), a 'short, stout-built, honest Highland figure' whose portrait appears in David Allan's famous painting *Highland Wedding at Blair Atholl* (1780), was unrivalled as a virtuoso performer of Scottish dance music. 'The livelier airs which belong to the class of what are called strathspey and reel . . . assumed in his hand a style of spirit, fire and beauty, which had never been heard before.' wrote a biographer, praising 'the effect of the sudden shout with which he frequently accompanied his playing in the quick tunes, and which seemed instantly to electrify the dancers, inspiring them with new life and energy, and rousing the spirits of the most inanimate.' The fiddler was paid £5 a year for his services to the Duke of Atholl and Raeburn's portrait of him, almost identical to the one in the Scottish National Portrait Gallery, can still be seen at Blair Castle, along with his fiddle, glass goblet and chair.

Gow had a reputation as a tippler and fittingly his favourite drink was whisky (*uisge beatha* – water of life). He composed the melody *Farewell to Whisky* in 1799 to express his sorrow at being deprived of the spirit on account of the poor barley crop – grain was prohibited for distilling that year. The tune is best played as a lament. The words are said to have been composed either by his son Nathaniel (1763–1831), a fashionable musician with a publishing business and musical instrument shop in Edinburgh, or his grandson Niel (1794–1823), who also composed and set poems to music. It appeared in *The Beauties of Gow*, one of their collections of Gow senior's works, published in 1819.

LORE

No region of Britain has a richer oral folk culture than the Gàidhealtachd, with its ceilidh-house tradition of story-telling and song, its prayers, incantations and rhythmic working songs. Charting the spirituality, superstitions and daily domestic rituals of traditional Highland life, this vernacular heritage of music, poetry and song developed in parallel to the classical Gaelic verse of the hereditary bards, whose literary tradition, as old as any in Western Europe, produced formally structured poetry with elaborate rhetorical codes. The sixteenth to eighteenth centuries were the great period of the Gaelic song-makers. Thanks to the collecting and recording of folklorists such as Alexander Carmichael, Frances Tolmie and Margaret Fay Shaw, a significant body of the oral folk repertoire of the Highlands and Hebrides has been preserved in print.

Tales of the Ceilidh House
(Sgeulachdan nan Taighean Cèilidh)

by **DONALD MACDONALD** (1926–2000)
(Dòmhnall Aonghais Bhàin)

Translated from the Gaelic by Ronald Black

Though the wind of the wolf-days* should blow
With all the keenness of a snell north wind,
Though the snow should stack against wall and the banks,
Though like steel it should lock on the top of the hills –
Nothing will keep us from the Ceilidh House
Where song, tale and rhyme will be heard.

Though rain should come ferociously in squalls,
Though sleet and hail hammer from the skies –
Nothing, not flood, nor deluge will hold me back!
Nor will there be tiredness or gloom about any one of us
When the stories begin – and from the seat by the fire
We hear the rich calm voice of the seanchaidh.†

The genealogy of our people will be uttered,
The history of clan and family recited.
There will be debate about the places and process
Of fishing, about the hardship and skill
Of the fisherman's art on the water –
Talk about mishaps and drownings at sea –
And remembrance of friends who the seas took from us.
[. . .]

---

* the Gaelic for January is *Am Faoilteach,* the month of the wolf
† a reciter/recorder of poetry and tales; historian

But better to me were the tales of the shielings
Where the young men and women learned music and song;
Where the cattle were tended on the summertime grasses
And herding was easy for the young as of old:
Unfenced was the sward where freedom was ours
And timeless the peace as we walked home to the fold.

But those days and the Ceilidh House are now in the past
New fashions and habits have forced change on the glens:
The old folk who sang in the houses I knew
Now moulder in earth they once trod so lightly.
New ways and new merriments have replaced the old ceilidh
And the houses of youth have long shut their doors.

Described by Ronald Black as 'the last of so many traditional poets from the area . . . the voice of the hills of Boisdale', Donald Macdonald lived at the foot of Easaval hill in South Uist in a cottage that survives, albeit decaying, as testament to a way of life that has now disappeared. Apart from a few periods employed away from home, he lived all his life here in South Lochboisdale, working the croft and collecting kelp for the alginate factory. At the little school he attended in a tin hut on the moor, he studied Shakespeare, Wordsworth, Byron and Shelley, and I well remember seeing a copy of Gibbon's *The Decline and Fall of the Roman Empire* lying on his windowsill. In 1997, when interviewed for Timothy Neat's book *The Voice of the Bard* (1999), he said 'poetry is the thing that has given me the greatest pleasure I have known'. Donald's 'free-flowing, well-wrought lyricism, love songs, elegantly expressed thoughts on death and change and some very funny works full of irony' are now widely admired. The house, which his father built in about 1920 with walls four feet thick and a thatched roof, was one of the 'ceilidh houses' known to every Gaelic community, and the poet remembered 'singing, talk, stories, from long before I went to school. We children and neighbours and friends all gathered, and I remember falling asleep to the music, or with the singing still loud in one ear. I liked the bagpipes and the accordion, now I listen to the wireless, which is very good'. There were plenty of bards in the vicinity when he was young. 'I myself was never a singer but I first started to make poems when I was at school or out at the herding'.

Peat-Fire Smooring Prayer
Translated from the Gaelic by Alexander Carmichael

The sacred Three
To save,
To shield,
To surround
The hearth,
The house,
The household
This eve,
This night,
Oh! This eve,
This night,
And every night,
Each single night.
Amen

This comes from the unrivalled collection of Gaelic hymns, songs, stories, incantations, customs and legends made by Alexander Carmichael (1832–1912) while touring the Highlands and Islands as an exciseman in the later nineteenth century. The cream of the collection was published (with his own translations from Gaelic) in his great work *Carmina Gadelica*, 'the biggest sum of literature in any Western European language handed down by word of mouth'.

Fire smooring, as the great folklorist noted, had more than just a practical purpose. 'The ceremony of smooring the fire is artistic and symbolic, and is performed with loving care. The embers are evenly spread on the hearth – which is generally in the middle of the floor – and formed into a circle. This circle is then divided into three equal sections, a small boss being left in the middle. A peat is laid between each section, each peat touching the boss, which forms a common centre. The first peat is laid down in name of the God of Life, the second in name of the God of Peace, the third in name of the God of Grace. The centre is then covered over with ashes sufficient to subdue but not to extinguish the fire in name of the Three of Light. The heap slightly raised in the centre is called 'Tulla nan Tri', the Hearth of the Three. When the smooring operation is complete, the woman closes her eyes, stretches her hand, and softly intones one of the many formulae current for these occasions.'

Loom Blessing

Translated from the Gaelic by Alexander Carmichael

Thrums nor odds of thread
My hand never kept, nor shall keep,

Every colour in the bow of the shower
Has gone through my fingers beneath the cross,

White and black, red and madder,
Green, dark grey, and scarlet,

Blue, and roan, and colour of the sheep,
And never a particle of cloth was wanting.

I beseech calm Bride the generous,
I beseech mild Mary the loving,

I beseech Christ Jesu the humane,
That I may not die without them,
    That I may not die without them.

'As you walk down the rugged road between the Black Houses your ears run the gauntlet of the shuttles' wrote Louis MacNeice, visiting Shawbost in Lewis in 1937. Even then, the majority of Hebridean cottages had a loom, and until relatively recently every domestic task was accompanied by a song, prayer or incantation. This blessing was collected orally from a Benbecula woman by Alexander Carmichael, who translated it from Gaelic.

Women were skilled at every stage of cloth making, from grading, washing, drying, teasing, oiling, carding and spinning the wool, soaking it in stale urine to stabilise it for dyeing and dyeing it with boiled crotal, heather, dulse, root of iris, dandelion, tormentil, bracken roots and other plants, earth or soot, to warping the loom, weaving the cloth and then shrinking it by waulking (fulling). When the cloth had been thoroughly cleaned in running water, laid out and dried, it was rolled up and turned three times sun-wise with a blessing on whoever might wear it.

A' Bhean Iadach

(The Jealous Woman)

Translated from the Gaelic by Margaret Fay Shaw, c.1932

THE WIFE: O! it was desire that sent me to the strand
             To pick dulse and gather limpets.
             'Girl over yonder beside the shore
             have you no pity for a young wife who is drowning?'

JEALOUS WOMAN: 'I have no pity, little do I care about her!'

THE WIFE: 'You will be established in my place;
             Stretch out your foot to me, stretch your hand to me.
             The corner of your plaid if you prefer it!
             Wretched to-night are my three children!
             One of them a year old, one two years,
             Another little one in need of being lulled to sleep!
             Little Iain, your mother's dearest,
             To-night you will not get your mother's breast;
             Though you got it, it would be of little good,
             Full it will be of salt water.
             Cold is my bed, wet with brine,
             Fortunate is the young woman who will go in my place,
             She will get wisdom, she will get modesty,
             She will get white hornless sheep,
             She will get cows in calf and heifers for bulling!
             The boat will come here to-morrow,
             My father and my three brothers will be on her,
             With good MacIntyre at the bow oar.
             They will find me after my drowning,
             My blue coat floating on the sea,
             My silver brooch on a stone beside me,
             And my beads around my neck;
             Hide it, hide it from my mother
             Until the sun rises to-morrow.'

Waulking songs (*òrain-luaidh*) were rhythmic accompaniments to
the task of waulking (or fulling) newly woven cloth. Continued in
some places until after the mid-twentieth century, waulking was
traditionally performed by women grouped around a long board,
thumping and beating the wet lengths of cloth to shrink it as it
circulated between them. The songs were usually long and often
picked up in speed and tempo as the physical action accelerated.

Typically, they told of love and death, birth, marriage and war, often with topical verses introduced. The traditional structure of the waulking song is lost in translation. In Gaelic, the verses sung by the soloist were couplets, the second line of each repeated as the first line of the next. These were punctuated by vocables (non-words, such as *Hùg ò* and *Huri a bhò*) sung by the group in the manner of a chorus.

Dating from the sixteenth century, *A' Bhean Iadach* was sung in various versions in the West Highlands and Hebrides. The tune and words of this one were taken down by Margaret Fay Shaw in South Uist in 1932. Though the song is of Scottish origin, the powerful motif of the jealous woman is shared by many European folktales and folksongs. The theme of two women in love with the same man is a universal one, here strongly assimilated into the Hebridean culture with its images of sea and seaweed, rocks and skerries, the tyranny of the tides. The jealous one entices the wife to the shore, leaving her to fall asleep and drown as the tide comes in. Just as she's about to be submerged, the wife wakes and begins to sing this song. Meanwhile, the jealous one usurps her place in the house and begins singing the very same song that she has heard on the lips of the drowning woman. And when the husband hears and comes to listen at the door, he understands the words and throws the imposter out of the house.

The Lewis Bridal Song

by **SIR HUGH ROBERTON** (1874–1952)

Step we gladly, on we go, heel for heel and toe for toe –
Arm and Arm and row on row, all for Mairi's wedding.

Over hillways up and down, myrtle green and bracken brown –
Past the shieling, thro' the town – all for sake of Mairi.

Red her cheeks as rowans are, bright her eye as any star,
Fairest o' them a' by far, is our darling Mairi.

Plenty herring, plenty meal, plenty peat to fill her creel,
Plenty bonnie bairns as weel; that's the toast for Mairi.

Though written by the composer/conductor Sir Hugh Roberton
(who also arranged the traditional melody for voice and piano) this
song conjures up something of the exhilarating rhythms of dancing
and music that accompanied a traditional Hebridean wedding. The
whole process, from betrothal to the days following the nuptuals,
was enshrined in custom and ceremony. About a week before the
wedding, the couple went about the district inviting neighbours to
their marriage feast, and this was followed by much singing, dancing
and piping as the wedding entertainment ensued. Eventually, the
guests formed a procession and everyone swung along singing and
piping as they conveyed the married couple to their new home,
whereupon the oldest member of the party broke a bannock over the
bride's head as she stepped over the threshold.

The Great Silkie

An earthly nourris sits and sings and, aye, she sings be lilly
   wean
'little ken I my bairny's father far less the land that he staps in.'

Then in steps he to her bed fit, And a grumley guest I'm sure
   was he;
Saying, 'Here I am, thy bairny's father, Although I be not
   comely.'

'I am a man upon the land, And I am a silkie in the sea.
And when I'm far and far from land, My home it is in Sule Skerry.'

'It was na' weel,' quo' the maiden fair, 'It was na' weel,' indeed
  quo' she.
'That the great silkie from Sule Skerry, Should hae come and
  brought a bairn ta me.'

Then he has taken a purse of gold, And he has pat it upon her
  knee,
Saying, 'Gie to me my little young son, And take thee up thy
  nourris fee.'

'And it shall come to pass on a simmer's day, When the sun
  shines het on ev'ra stane,
That I shall tak my little young son, And teach him for tae swim
  the faem.'

'And thou shall marry a proud gunner, And a richt guid gunner
  I'm sure he'll be,
But the vera first shot that ere he'll shoot, He'll kill baith my
  young son and me.'

'Alas, alas,' the maiden cried, 'This weary fate that's laid on me'
And ance she sobbed and ance she sighed, And her tender heart
  did brak in three.

Who has not heard the grey seals of the Atlantic singing with human
voices as they lie on the rocks? Silkies, or selkies, are seals that shed
their skins and become human. Shetland and Orkney lore is
particularly rich in stories about selkies, and there are similar
legends in Ireland, Wales and the Faroe Isles. A selkie can only make
contact with a human for a brief time before it must slide back into
the sea. Often, the human does not know that their lover is a selkie
and wakes to find it gone. But sometimes a human will hide the skin
to prevent the selkie returning to seal form. Male selkies are very
handsome in human form and powerfully seductive to women.

They tend to seek out those who are dissatisfied with their romantic life, or married women waiting for their fishermen husbands to return. If a woman wishes to make contact with a selkie, she must go down to the shore and shed seven tears into the sea. Female selkies are no less attractive to men and are said to make excellent wives, although they are often to be seen gazing longingly at their true home, the sea. There are various versions of this Orcadian ballad, which tells of a Norwegian girl whose child was fathered by a selkie from Sule Skerry (40 miles west of Orkney).

VERSES FROM *Lullaby*

Translated from the Gaelic by Alexander Carmichael

The nest of the raven
Is in the hawthorn rock,
   My little one will sleep and
      he shall have the bird.

The nest of the skylark
Is in the track of 'Dubhag', [a cow]
   My little one will sleep and
      he shall have the bird.

The nest of the lapwing
Is in the hummocked marsh,
   My little one will sleep and
      he shall have the bird.

The nest of the kite
Is high on the mountain-slope,
   My little one will sleep and
      he shall have the bird.

The nest of the plover
Is in the wooded copse,
   My little one will sleep and
      he shall have the bird.

The nest of the starling
Is under the wing of the thatch,
   My little one will sleep and
      he shall have the bird.

The nest of the curlew
Is in the bubbling peat-moss,
   My little one will sleep and
      he shall have the bird.

The nest of the oyster-catcher
Is among the smooth shingles,
   My little one will sleep and
      he shall have the bird.

LOVE

Though inspired by the spellbinding romance of the Highland landscape and haunted by the lyrical poetry of Highland places and place names, the sentiments expressed in these poems transcend any geographical boundary. Here is love in its many moods, from rapture on first sight and celebration of love, to longing and waiting, uncertainty, absence and yearning, and the doomed love of tragedy and despair.

FROM *Fragments of Ancient Poetry collected in the Highlands of Scotland, and translated from the Gaelic or Erse Language* (1760)

by **JAMES MACPHERSON** (1736–96)

Vinvela

My love is a son of the hill. He pursues the flying deer. His gray dogs are panting round him; his bow-strings sound in the wind. Whether by the fount of the rock, or by the stream of the mountain thou liest; when the rushes are nodding with the wind, and the mist is flying over thee, let me approach my love unperceived, and see him from the rock. Lovely I saw thee first by the aged oak of Branno; thou wert returning tall from the chace; the fairest among thy friends.

Shilric

What voice is that I hear? that voice like the summer-wind. – I sit not by the nodding rushes; I hear not the fount of the rock. Afar, Vinvela, afar I go to the wars of Fingal. My dogs attend me no more. No more I tread the hill. No more from on high I see thee, fair-moving by the stream of the plain; bright as the bow of heaven; as the moon on the western wave. .

Vinvela

Then thou are gone, O Shilric! and I am alone on the hill. The deer are seen on the brow; void of fear they graze along. No more they dread the wind; no more the rustling tree. The hunter is far removed; he is in the field of graves. Strangers! sons of the waves! spare my lovely Shilric.

[. . .]

James Macpherson grew up in Gaelic-speaking Badenoch in the violent aftermath of Culloden. Raised in the culture of the ceilidh house, he acquired a classical education at Aberdeen University, after which he became acquainted with the Edinburgh literati while working as a tutor. Macpherson travelled as far as the Hebrides collecting ancient manuscripts and oral verse, which he then reworked, embellished and translated into English, publishing the results as genuine material handed down from the third century warrior-bard Ossian, son of Fingal. Despite widespread speculation over their authenticity, these publications were hugely successful, partly because of the way they bridged the sensibilities of the Enlightenment and Romantic movements, offering at a time of great preoccupation with national identity a home-grown origin mythology and bardic tradition to rival those of the ancient Greeks. They made Macpherson extremely successful – rich enough to commission Robert Adam to design him a Highland seat and famous enough to be buried at Westminster Abbey.

He believed that Highlanders, isolated from the corrupting influences of urbanised society, were the last relics of the ancient Celts. But even the Highlands were in decline, and *Fragments of Ancient Poetry* (a series of short prose poems presented as episodes from a greater lost work) has been interpreted as an eighteenth-century lament on the passing of an older, better order. Certainly the theme of sorrow is sustained; this excerpt from Fragment I comes from the doomed tale of Vinvela and her huntsman warrior Shilric.

The Solitary Reaper

by **WILLIAM WORDSWORTH** (1770–1850)

1805

Behold her, single in the field,
Yon solitary Highland Lass!
Reaping and singing by herself;
Stop here, or gently pass!
Alone she cuts and binds the grain,
And sings a melancholy strain;
O listen! For the Vale profound
Is overflowing with the sound.

No Nightingale did ever chaunt
More welcome notes to weary bands
Of travellers in some shady haunt,
Among Arabian sands:
A voice so thrilling ne'er was heard
In spring-time from the Cuckoo-bird,
Breaking the silence of the seas
Among the farthest Hebrides.

Will no one tell me what she sings? –
Perhaps the plaintive numbers flow
For old, unhappy, far-off things,
And battles long ago:
Or is it some more humble lay,
Familiar matter of to-day?
Some natural sorrow, loss, or pain,
That has been, and may be again?

Whate'er the theme, the Maiden sang
As if her song could have no ending;
I saw her singing at her work,
And o'er the sickle bending; –
I listened, motionless and still;
And, as I mounted up the hill,
The music in my heart I bore,
Long after it was heard no more.

One of Wordsworth's most haunting lyrics, this poem was composed between 1803, when he made a tour of Scotland with his sister Dorothy, and 1805, when he decided to publish another volume of small poems. Interestingly, although the pastoral scene described so entrancingly would have been common in the Highlands at the time, Wordsworth actually got the idea from his friend Thomas Wilkinson's manuscript for *A Tour of Scotland* (1787), which includes the following passage: 'Passed by a Female who was reaping alone, she sung in Erse as she bended over her sickle, the sweetest human voice I ever heard. Her strains were tenderly melancholy, and felt delicious long after they were heard no more'.

Lord Ullin's Daughter

by **THOMAS CAMPBELL** (1777–1844)

1804

A chieftain to the Highlands bound,
Cries, 'Boatman, do not tarry!
And I'll give ye a silver pound
To row us o'er the ferry!'

'Now who be ye would cross Lochgyle,
This dark and stormy water?'
'Oh, I'm the chief of Ulva's isle,
And this Lord Ullin's daughter. –

'And fast before her father's men
Three days we've fled together,
For should he find us in the glen,
My blood would stain the heather.

'His horsemen hard behind us ride;
Should they our steps discover,
Then who will cheer my bonny bride
When they have slain her lover?' –

Out spoke the hardy Highland wight,
'I'll go, my chief – I'm ready;
It is not for your silver bright;
But for your winsome lady.

'And by my word! the bonny bird
In danger shall not tarry:
So though the waves are raging white,
I'll row you o'er the ferry.' –

By this the storm grew loud apace,
The water-wraith was shrieking;
And in a scowl of Heaven each face
Grew dark as they were speaking.

But still as louder blew the wind,
And as the night grew drearer,
Adown the glen rode armed men,
Their trampling sounded nearer. –

'Oh haste thee, haste!' the lady cries,
'Though tempests round us gather;
I'll meet the raging of the skies,
But not an angry father.' –

The boat has left a stormy land,
A stormy sea before her, –
When, oh! too strong for human hand
The tempest gathered o'er her.

And still they rowed amidst the roar
Of waters fast prevailing:
Lord Ullin reached that fatal shore,
His wrath was changed to wailing. –

For sore dismayed, through storm and shade,
His child he did discover: –
One lovely hand she stretched for aid,
And one was round her lover.

'Come back! Come back!' he cried in grief,
Across the stormy water:
'And I'll forgive your Highland chief,
My daughter! – oh, my daughter!' –

'Twas vain: the loud waves lashed the shore,
Return or aid preventing:
The waters wild went o'er his child,
And he was left lamenting.

Thomas Campbell is best remembered for rousing battle songs such as *Ye Mariners of England*, *The Battle of the Baltic* and *Hohenlinden*, and for his romantic ballads. Although not his best, I have to include this one as a particular favourite that we as children could recite by heart, stirred by its tragic events. Campbell (who later settled in London) must have visited Ulva, the island off Mull at the mouth of Loch na Keal (Lochgyle), while working as a tutor to the Campbells of Sunipol in 1795. There he would have heard about Allan Maclean of Knock, who refused to give his daughter's hand in marriage to the chief of Ulva. The thwarted couple therefore escaped through the hills and set off by boat for Ulva from the southern shore of Loch na Keal. The boat is believed to have foundered on a rock between Inch Kenneth and Eilean Eòrsa. Their bodies were washed ashore on the Mull coast below Oskamull and a Celtic cross now marks the site of their graves.

Eriskay Love Lilt

(Gradh Geal Mo Chridh)

Translated from the Gaelic

Bheir me o, horo van o
Bheir me o, horo van ee
Bheir me o, o horo ho
Sad am I, without thee.

Thou'rt the music of my heart;
Harp of joy, o cruit mo chridh;
Moon of guidance by night;
Strength and light thou'rt to me.
Chorus

In the morning, when I go
To the white and shining sea,
In the calling of the seals
Thy soft calling to me.
Chorus

When I'm lonely, dear white heart,
Black the night and wild the sea,
By love's light, my foot finds
The old pathway to me.
Chorus

The drawing room rendition of this Hebridean song, recorded from Mary MacInnes of Eriskay, was the creation of Marjory Kennedy-Fraser (1857–1930) who, in collaboration with the Revd Kenneth Macleod, collected and translated traditional Gaelic songs and arranged them for voice, piano and clarsach (harp), publishing them in three volumes between 1909 and 1921 – their famous *Songs of the Hebrides*. The little island of Eriskay, which lies between Barra and South Uist (connected to the latter by a causeway since 2001), is famous for being the place where Bonnie Prince Charlie first set foot on British soil in 1745.

Message to Gavin

by KATHLEEN RAINE (1908–2003)

1969

Leaving you, I have come to Iona's strand
Where the far is near, and the dear, far.
Ardnamurchan's sea-dragon that guarded our south
Now bars the north with its stony jaw;
Staffa a barren rock across the sound
That seemed a mirage shimmering from some unreal land.

Eigg, Rhum and the Cuillin faded to a thin veil;
My eyes retrace the lines of long familiar hills
To find you beyond that texture of dream,
Absence is too hard for the remembering heart to learn –
I walk on your most distant shore:
One horizon enrings us still.

A dazzle of light on your sun's ocean path,
A hidden rock where the white surf foams,
The faintest feather of cloud in your sky –
Since not again can I be with you life with life
I would be with you as star with distant star,
As drop of water in the one bright bitter sea.

Gavin Maxwell, most famous as the author of *Ring of Bright Water*, lived on the West coast of Scotland from the 1940s until his death in 1969 and many of the episodes in his relationship with the writer Kathleen Raine took place in this remote and ruggedly beautiful setting. In 1950, after Maxwell had allowed her to stay at his home Sandaig (the Camusfeàrna of *Ring of Bright Water*) in his absence, she wrote 'Living in his house, seeing his sky over me, the spaces of his sea, those near hills and far mountains which were the regions of his imagination . . . I lived like Psyche in the house of love, alone yet not alone. In the pool of his waterfall I bathed, on his beaches I gathered shells and stones written with the strange language of the sea.'

But, as Douglas Botting reveals in his wonderful biography, *Gavin Maxwell A Life* (1993), their friendship was tempestuous. On one occasion, in July 1956, Maxwell arrived home not expecting to find her there and ordered her to leave immediately; devastated, she went out later that night into a storm. 'There, halfway between the bridge over the burn and the house, stood the rowan tree. Beside herself with anguish and weeping aloud, she laid her hands on the trunk and called upon the tree for justice. 'Let Gavin suffer, in this place, as I am suffering now!' she cried.' When Sandaig was destroyed by fire in January 1968, Kathleen Raine blamed herself because of this curse.

This is the last of her Platonic love poems inspired by Maxwell and his Scottish paradise. It was written on Iona, a fortnight or so after she had bid farewell to him at the end of a 'volcanic' visit to his final home on Eilean Bàn. They had quarrelled on her last evening and he was already ill; the concluding lines suggest that she will never see him again.

Shores

by **SORLEY MACLEAN** (1911–1996)
(Somhairle MacGill-Eain)

*c.*1940
Translated from the Gaelic by the poet

If we were in Talisker on the shore
where the great white mouth
opens between two hard jaws
Rubha nan Clach and the Bioda Ruadh,
I would stand beside the sea
re-newing love in my spirit
while the ocean was filling
Talisker bay forever:
I would stand there on the bareness of the shore
until Prishal bowed his stallion head.

And if we were together
on Calgary shore in Mull,
between Scotland and Tiree,
between the world and eternity,
I would stay there till doom
measuring sand, grain by grain,
and in Uist, on the shore of Homhsta
in presence of that wide solitude,
I would wait there for ever,
for the sea draining drop by drop.

And if I were on the shore of Moidart
with you, for whom my care is new,

I would put up in a synthesis of love for you
the ocean and the sand, drop and grain.
And if we were on Mol Stenscholl Staffin
when the unhappy surging sea dragged
the boulders and threw them over us,
I would build the rampart wall
against an alien eternity grinding.

'The phenomenon of MacLean', wrote Iain Crichton Smith, 'is that he seems to be able to cross linguistic boundaries and to have an effect on those who know no Gaelic and this in spite of the fact that he believes that Gaelic poetry cannot be translated into English, since the genius of the two languages is so different'. Even in English this poem, with its beautiful resonance of place names recited in the medieval tradition, conveys something of the bare, powerful, lyrical passion of Sorley MacLean's love poetry.

Fear a' Bhàta
(The Boatman)
Translated from the Gaelic by Kenneth Hurlstone Jackson

There are several versions in English of this Gaelic love song; this one from Kenneth Jackson's A Celtic Miscellany reads better, but Lachlan MacBean's late nineteenth-century version (heard, for example, in the folksinger Sandy Denny's haunting rendition, accessible on-line) fits better with the beautiful melody. The song is said to have been composed in the late 18th century by Jane Finlayson of Tong on the Isle of Lewis. Her boatman was Donald MacRae, a young fisherman from Uig whom she later married.

From the highest hill I look out often
to try if I can see the Boatman;
come you to-day, or come you to-morrow?
And sad am I if you come never.

Oh, the Boatman, na hóro eile,
oh, the Boatman, na hóro eile,
oh, the Boatman, na hóro eile,
my long farewell where you may go to.

My heart within is bruised and broken
and from my eyes the tears are streaming;
come you to-night, shall I expect you,
or shut the door with heavy sighing?

Oh, the Boatman, etc.

Often then I ask the boatmen
if they have seen you, if you're in safety;
but every one of them is saying
that if I love you I am foolish.

Oh, the Boatman, etc.

Though they said that you are fickle
that did not lessen my fondness for you;
you are my dreaming in the night time,
and in the morning I'm seeking for you.

Oh, the Boatman, etc.

All my friends unceasing tell me
that I must forget your image,
but their advice is just as idle
as to dam the tide when it is flowing.

Oh, the Boatman, etc.

Marry the Lass

by **ANDREW GREIG** (b.1951)

Published 1973

Body black in the rock spine of Quinag
the thought intrudes: marry the lass?

Easy to spend a lifetime
with the minimum of fuss and sunny days …

He dismisses the thought, and the day
is spent struggling with unyielding rock.

Through evening the return is made,
fingers loose, grey eyes on the far Atlantic –

Also recalling her mother's ballooning outlines.
Home again. The piratical poet

Decides they will instead enjoy the
fashionable fruit of living in sin,

And muttering defiantly 'Many good years yet',
takes his boots off, has a dram, forgets the matter.

One of the things that draws me to the work of this Scottish poet, novelist and travel writer is the way he takes timeless themes and historical situations and views them through the prism of gritty contemporary reality. A love of adventure and romance permeates Andrew Greig's writings and mountaineering, that key influence in the Highlands since the nineteenth century, has been one of his great passions. His climbing experiences, both at home and among the highest mountain ranges in the world, have inspired a number of his books and poems.

LIGHT

What is it that makes the quality of light in these northern landscapes so bewitching? Is it the raking weather, the long summer days, the lack of pollution in the air, the reflecting waters? Light, illuminated from sky or lamp, assumes a symbolic presence in each of these poems.

Gloaming

by **KATHLEEN JAMIE** (b.1962)

Published 2004

We are flying, this summer's night, toward a brink, a wire-thin
rim of light. It swells as we descend, then illuminates the land
enough to let us name, by hill or river mouth, each township below.
This is the North, where people, the world perhaps likes to imagine,
hold a fish in one hand, in the other a candle.
I could settle for that. The plane shudders, then rolls to a standstill
at the far end of the runway. It's not day, this light we've entered,
but day is present at the negotiation. The sky's the still
pale grey of a heron, attending the tide-pools of the shore.

Born in the west of Scotland, Kathleen Jamie now lives in Fife and
lectures in Creative Writing at St Andrews University; she is
regarded as one of the best Scottish poets living today. A slightly
different version of this poem was published as *The Heron* in 2002.

Harris, East Side

by NORMAN MACCAIG (1910–1996)

Published 1965

Stones crowd and shine
As though a Christ preached, they his multitude.
(Weather's their gospel, and they need no sign).

The narrow bay
Has a knuckle of houses and a nail of sand
By which the sea hangs grimly to the land.

A boat, deflowered
Of its brown sail, pokes its bald pistil up,
Flattening the seed of miles it has devoured.

It rocks upon
The rocking world and sends its small waves back
Against the waves that turned its blue to black.

On a green sward
A woman stands kneedeep in hens and from
A flashing pail scatters their peaceful Word.

Around altars hung
With holy weeds, ducks, as they skid and lurch,
Quack soft, like laymen working in a church.

And light bends down
In seeming benediction, though it comes
From where hail buds and vicious thunder drums.

Its storms lie round,
Already here where a roof shows its bones
Or where a child sits in a field of stones.

'The east coast is of a bolder character ... barren, hilly, and almost uninhabited' wrote William Daniell, visiting Harris in 1815. The remarkable lunar landscape of the Bays district was virtually devoid of permanent occupation until a string of townships sprang up around the harbours and piers built by Macleod of Harris to serve his fishing and kelping enterprises in the late eighteenth century. These settlements on land forged from the world's oldest rock swelled to a state of impossible overcrowding in the nineteenth century as widespread evictions depopulated the fertile west coast. Many of those who did not emigrate formed remote coastal weaving and crofting townships such as Plocrapool, linked by the tortuous 'Golden Road' only in 1947. The landscape bears testimony to their struggle for survival: every tillable slope and small, sour patch of soil is seamed with *feannagan,* the Hebridean cultivation rigs known as 'lazy beds'. And, stern as the landscape, the people's Presbyterian religion remains their rockbed.

Island

by **KENNETH STEVEN** (b.1968)

Published 2007

I remember what it was like to barefoot that house,
Wood rooms bleached by light. Days were new voyages, journeys,
Coming home a pouring out of stories and of starfish.
The sun never died completely in the night,
The skies just turned luminous, the wind
Tugged at the strings in the grass like a hand
In a harp. I did not sleep, too glad to listen by a window
To the sorrow sounds of the birds
As they swept down in skeins, and rose again, celebrating

All that was summer. I did not sleep, the weight of school
Behind and before too great to waste a grain of this.
One four in the morning at first larksong I went west over the
    dunes,
Broke down running onto three miles of white shell sand, and
    stood.
A wave curled and silked the shore in a single seamless breath.
I went naked into the water, ran deep into a green
Through which I was translucent. I rejoiced
In something I could not name; I celebrated a wonder
Too huge to hold. I trailed home, slow and golden,
Dried by the sunlight.

This poem is a memory from a holiday on the island of Coll, where
the poet spent several summers with his family as a teenager in the
mid-1980s. It evokes those memories that many of us cherish of
island holidays . . . favourite places visited year after year that
remain unchanged and ever gilded in our imaginations. Kenneth
Steven has since published numerous poems and novels which
have been translated into many languages. His latest collection of
poetry, *Island*, was published in 2009.

The Northern Islands

by EDWIN MUIR (1887–1959)

1953

In favoured summers
These islands have the sun all to themselves
And light a toy to play with, weeks on end.

The empty sky and waters are a shell
Endlessly turning, turning the wheel of light,
While the tranced waves run wavering up the sand.
The beasts sleep when they can, midnight or midday,
Slumbering on into unending brightness.
The green, green fields give too much, are too rank
With beautiful beasts for breeding or for slaughter.
The horses, glorious useless race, are leaving.
Have the old ways left with them, and the faith,
Lost in this dream too comfortable and goodly
To make room for a blessing? Where can it fall?
The old ways change in the turning, turning light,
Taking and giving life to life from life.

The son of an Orkney farming family, Edwin Muir moved to Glasgow when he was fourteen, where the experience of modern capitalism, urban squalor and his family's early deaths brought him close to mental breakdown. He became a Socialist, married in 1919 and moved to London, soon after which he began writing poetry seriously and making his living as a critic and a reviewer. From 1942 to 1950 he worked for the British Council in Edinburgh, Prague and Rome. He then became warden of Newbattle Abbey College, where he taught George Mackay Brown, before settling near Cambridge in his final years.

Muir sent this and another poem to George Mackay Brown in Orkney on 31 March 1953. 'They're not very like my other poems' he wrote, 'at least as far as I can judge'. This one was published in *New Statesman* on 26 June 1953.

Rackwick

by **GEORGE MACKAY BROWN** (1921–96)

Published 1954

Let no tongue idly whisper here.
Between those strong red cliffs,
Under that great mild sky
Lies Orkney's last enchantment,
The hidden valley of light.
Sweetness from the clouds pouring,
Songs from the surging sea.
Fenceless fields, fishermen with ploughs
And old heroes, endlessly sleeping
In Rackwick's compassionate hills.

Rackwick left a deep impression on George Mackay Brown when he visited it for the first time on a trip to Hoy in the summer of 1946. 'The beauty of Rackwick struck me like a blow' he wrote, and, as Maggie Fergusson describes so eloquently in her brilliant biography, the sea valley was to become a source of inexhaustible inspiration. Haunted by its beauty but also by its tragedy – Rackwick had once been home to a thriving community and was now all but abandoned – George Mackay Brown wrote about it at length – in, for example, *An Orkney Tapestry* (1969) and *Let's See the Orkney Islands* (1948). 'But the fairest region of all Hoy is the valley of Rackwick, which lies, shut in with mountains, on the north-west coast of the island … indeed, on a still summer evening, with invisible larks spilling enchantment into the valley, the magic of Rackwick has power to bind a man's heart for ever'.

The Light-Keeper

by **ROBERT LOUIS STEVENSON** (1850–94)

1869–70

1

The brilliant kernel of the night,
The flaming lightroom circles me:
I sit within a blaze of light
Held high above the dusky sea.
Far off the surf doth break and roar
Along bleak miles of moonlit shore,
Where through the tides the tumbling wave
Falls in an avalanche of foam
And drives its churnèd waters home
Up many an undercliff and cave.

The clear bell chimes: the clockworks strain:
The turning lenses flash and pass,
Frame turning within glittering frame
With frosty gleam of moving glass:
Unseen by me, each dusky hour
The sea-waves welter up the tower
Or in the ebb subside again;
And ever and anon all night,
Drawn from afar by charm of light,
A sea-bird beats against the pane.

And lastly when dawn ends the night
And belts the semi-orb of sea,
The tall, pale pharos in the light

Looks white and spectral as may be.
The early ebb is out: the green
Straight belt of sea-weed now is seen,
That round the basement of the tower
Marks out the interspace of tide;
And watching men are heavy-eyed,
And sleepless lips are dry and sour.

The night is over like a dream:
The sea-birds cry and dip themselves;
And in the early sunlight, steam
The newly-bared and dripping shelves,
Around whose verge the glassy wave
With lisping wash is heard to lave;
While, on the white tower lifted high,
With yellow light in faded glass
The circling lenses flash and pass,
And sickly shine against the sky.

2

As the steady lenses circle
With a frosty gleam of glass;
And the clear bell chimes,
And the oil brims over the lip of the burner,
Quiet and still at his desk,
The lonely light-keeper
Holds his vigil.

Lured from afar,
The bewildered sea-gull beats
Dully against the lantern;
Yet he stirs not, lifts not his head
From the desk where he reads,

Lifts not his eyes to see
The chill blind circle of night
Watching him through the panes.
This is his country's guardian,
The outmost sentry of peace.
This is the man,
Who gives up all that is lovely in living
For the means to live.

Poetry cunningly gilds
The life of the light-keeper,
Held on high in the blackness
In the burning kernel of night.
The seaman sees and blesses him.
The Poet, deep in a sonnet,
Numbers his inky fingers
Fitly to praise him.
Only we behold him,
Sitting, patient and stolid,
Martyr to a salary.

Many of the lighthouses that pinpoint the treacherous reefs and
rocks off the Scottish coast were built by the famous Stevensons, the
family to which Robert Louis Stevenson belonged. During his three-
year engineering apprenticeship around the time that *The Light-
Keeper* was written, the poet visited a number of their graceful towers
in the Highlands and Islands, including Alan Stevenson's Skerryvore
off Tiree of 1844, and the shore works for D. & T. Stevenson's Dhu
Heartach off Mull, then under construction. Did he have a particular
light in mind when he wrote this poem? It describes a rock light, of
which there are only very few in Scotland. 'Far off the surf doth break
and roar/Along bleak miles of moonlit shore' says the light-keeper,

which does not rule out Dhu Heartach. But the 'straight belt of sea-weed ... round the basement of the tower' could apply to Skerryvore or his grandfather Robert Stevenson's Bell Rock of 1811 after a Spring tide. Or perhaps he was just using poetic licence. Though Stevenson loved the outdoor and seafaring aspects of engineering, he realised in 1871 that he had no interest in pursuing the profession and decided to concentrate on literature instead.

Acknowledgements

I would like to thank the following for their help during the preparation of this collection: Kitty Turley, Maggie Fergusson, Alan Riach, Sarah Fraser, Rose Baring, Hugh Cheape, Paul McCallum Angus Nicol, Ronald Black and the Scottish Poetry Library.

I would also like to thank all of the authors for making this collection possible by allowing us to use their material, and gratefully acknowledge permission to reprint copyright material as follows:

The Literary Estate of George Mackay Brown for permissions to use 'Roads', 'Rackwick', 'The Kirk and the Ship' and 'Hamnavoe', all by the poet; The Canna Collections and the National Trust for Scotland, for permission to use 'Moladh Uibhist' and 'A' Bhean Iadach', both translated from the Gaelic by Margaret Fay Shaw; Derick Thomson for permissions to use 'St Columba's Isle' from *Creachadh na Clàrsaich* and 'Everlasting Sailing' from *Sùil air Fàire*; David Higham Associates for permission to use an extract from 'The Hebrides' by Louis MacNeice, published in *Collected Poems* by Faber & Faber; Polygon, an imprint of Birlinn Ltd, for permission to reproduce 'Harris, East Side' and 'A Man in Assynt' from *The Poems of Norman MacCaig* by Norman MacCaig; Brian Keeble for permission to reproduce 'Message to Gavin' from *Collected Poems* by Kathleen Raine; Kenneth Steven for permission to reproduce 'Island' from *Wildscape*; Julia Wigan for permission to use 'The River'; Felicity Henderson for permission to reproduce 'Ballad of the Men of Knoydart' by Hamish Henderson; Ronald Black for permission to use his translations of 'Moladh Beinn Dòbhrain' by Duncan Bàn Macintyre from his book *An Lasair* 'Tales of the Ceilidh House' by Donald Macdonald from *Smuaintean fo Éiseabhal* and 'An Ataireached Àrd by Donald MacIver from *An Tuil*; Meg Bateman, for permission to use 'Happiness'; Andrew Greig, for permission to use 'Marry the Lass' from his collection *White Boats*; Carcanet Press Limited for permission to use 'Gannet' and 'Midge' by Edwin Morgan, both from *Virtual and Other Realities*, 'Canedolia', also by Edwin Morgan, from *Collected Poems*, 'The Clearances', 'The White Air of March' by Iain Crichton Smith, from his *Collected Poems*, and 'Gaelic Stories' from *Burn is Aran*, 'Hallaig' and 'Shores' by Sorley Maclean from *From Wood to Ridge* and four poems by Hugh MacDiarmid, 'The Birlinn of Clanranald', 'Perfect', 'Scotland Small?' and 'The Little White Rose', all from his *Complete Poems*; Thomas Owen Clancy for allowing us to publish his translation of 'Last Verse in Praise of St Columba' originally published in *Iona: the earliest poetry of a Celtic Monastery*, by Edinburgh University Press; the Literary Estate of John Lorne Campbell for permission to use his translation of 'The Proud Plaid' by Alasdair Mac Mhaighstir Alasdair; Canongate and the Literary Estate of Naomi Mitchison for permission to use 'Wester Ross' from *The Cleansing of the Knife*; Faber & Faber for permission to use 'Rannoch, by Glencoe' by T S Eliot, 'St Kilda's Parliament' by Douglas Dunn and 'The Northern Islands' by Edwin Muir; Edinburgh University Press for permission to reprint 'The Daft Hill Plover' by George Campbell Hay and Picador for permission to reprint Kathleen Jamie's 'Gloaming'.

Every effort has been made to trace or contact copyright holders. The publishers would be pleased to rectify any omissions brought to their notice at the earliest opportunity.

Index of First Lines

Index of Poem Titles

Index of Poets